YOU CERTAINLY COULDN'T MAKE IT UP

Jack Crossley spent some 40 years in Fleet Street, first as a reporter on the *Daily Mail* and later as news editor/assistant editor on the *Mail*, the *Observer*, the *Herald* (Glasgow), the *Daily Express*, *The Times* and, for two crazy months, the *National Enquirer* in Florida.

He also edited the *Sunday Standard*, a short-lived quality broadsheet in Scotland, and was briefly a reporter on the Quincy *Patriot Ledger* in Massachusetts.

He now lives in London with his wife, Kate.

YOU CERTAINLY
COULDN'T
MAKE IT UP

YOU CERTAINLY COULDN'T MAKE IT UP

Yet more bizarre-but-true stories from around Britain

JOHN BLAKE

For Hannah and Amy

Published by John Blake Publishing Ltd,
3 Bramber Court, 2 Bramber Road,
London W14 9PB, England

www.blake.co.uk

First published in paperback in 2007

ISBN 978 1 84454 476 9

British Library Cataloguing-in-Publication Data:

A catalogue record for this book is available from the British Library.

Design by www.envydesign.co.uk
Illustrations by Gary Crossley
Printed in the UK by CPI Bookmarque, Croydon, CR0 4TD

1 3 5 7 9 10 8 6 4 2

Papers used by John Blake Publishing are natural, recyclable
products made from wood grown in sustainable forests. The
manufacturing processes conform to the environmental regulations of
the country of origin.

CONTENTS

INTRODUCTION

A family came across three boxes while sorting through the effects of a deceased relative. One was labelled Long Pieces of String. Another was labelled Short Pieces of String. A third was labelled Pieces of String Too Short to Keep. This piece of nonsense got me started on the hunt for similar items buried in the mountain of newspapers I read as part of my day job. Originally, I wanted to call the first volume *Pieces of String Too Short to Keep*. But the brains that power John Blake Publishing howled with mocking derision and won the best of three falls in the battle to have the book called *You Couldn't Make it Up* in 2003. This was followed by *You Really Couldn't Make it Up* in 2004, *You Absolutely Couldn't Make it Up* in 2005 and *You Positively Couldn't Make it Up* in 2006.

Compiling the books has become a family affair. I find the items, my son Gary sorts them into sensible order, my son Andrew provides the cartoons, my wife Kate is the pre-publication critic: if she doesn't laugh – or at least smile – at a particular item then that item gets the chop. Another important group is the regulars at the Blue Peter, my local pub in Polperro, Cornwall. They have a keen eye for the kind of stuff I am looking for and that explains why the *Western Morning News* finds it way into my collection. Anybody can join in. Readers of this book can send in their own choice cuttings to John Blake Publishing. Please make sure the cuttings are dated and the publication identified.

Jack Crossley
September 2007

Chapter 1

SIGNS OF THE TIMES

Warning on a pack of Tesco Scottish salmon: 'Allergy advice – contains fish.'

Independent on Sunday

Warning sign on a children's badge: 'Sharp point. Not suitable for children under three.' This was on a badge carrying the proud message: 'I am 2.'

Financial Times

'The Oldham Branch of the RSPCA is offering free neutering and spaying to anyone on benefits.'

Elizabeth Garside, of Oldham, Lancashire,
Oldham Evening Chronicle

'Desk suitable for lady with thick legs and large drawers.'

Classified ad in the
Leicester Mercury

A sign by a river in Selby, Yorkshire, reads: 'RIVER RESCUE. In the event of falling into river, dial 999, ask for Police/Fire, indicating you need river rescue.'
Spotted by Hilary Gigg of Hambleton, North Yorkshire,
Daily Mail

Mary Curtis, of Oxford, reports an instruction which comes with a travel hairdryer:
'Do not use while sleeping.'

Daily Mail

Roy Hyde of Cheltenham writes of an American colleague being startled by a sign saying 'Maidenhead Bypass'. He couldn't imagine what the device might be used for – and wondered if there would be a market for it back home.

The Times

Roy Hyde's American colleague reminded Douglas MacDonald, of Norwich, of Americans being puzzled by posters proclaiming: 'Enjoy the Norfolk Broads.'

The Times

Sylvie Ewen, of Haywards Heath, West Sussex, was relieved that the bunch of bananas she bought had a label saying 'great when peeled'. 'Phew,' she writes. 'Narrow escape. I could have choked on the skins.'

Daily Telegraph

Cyclists in Penarth, near Cardiff, were perturbed by a roadwork sign in English and Welsh. The English version said 'CYCLISTS DISMOUNT.' The Welsh version was 'LLD Y BLEDREN DYMCHWELYD', which means 'Your bladder disease has returned'. A computer translation, confusing the words cyclists and cystitis, was blamed for the mistake.

Penarth Times

Election poster spotted in Ireland: 'VOTE FOR O'BRIEN. O'FLAHERTY WILL GET YOU NOWHERE.'

J. Hughes of Waltham Cross, Hertfordshire,
Reader's Digest

The *London Review of Books* carries some hilarious lonely heart ads, and Christina Odone was tickled by one from a man lumbered with a second mortgage who was seeking a woman 'with active credit cards'.

Daily Telegraph

Postmen and women were given cameras to photograph the weird and wonderful signs they come across on their rounds. Here are some of the results published in a book called *Unseen UK*, with proceeds going to the Help the Hospices charity:

- WARNING [alongside a picture of a fierce guard dog]. I can make it to the fence in 2.8 seconds. CAN YOU?
- Sod the dog. Beware of the kids.
- CAUTION. Free-range children and animals.
- We shoot every tenth sales person calling here. The ninth just left.

Daily Mail

A competition with a cash prize was organised to find a name for Fort William's new health centre. After sifting through many suggestions the chosen winner was:

FORT WILLIAM HEALTH CENTRE

Duncan Campbell's Diary in the *Guardian*

Bill Day, of Horley, Surrey, spotted this in a clearinghouse catalogue:

- 41-piece knife set
- Stainless steel blades resist wear and never need sharpening
- Free knife sharpener when you buy the set

Daily Mail

4

For thirty years the villagers of Elmswell, Suffolk, campaigned to get a road sign directing lorry drivers to a nearby bacon factory. They got it in June 2006 – the day before the factory closed down.

Daily Telegraph

Upsetting for pet lovers? Road sign seen outside Weymouth: 'Cats' eyes removed.'

Guardian

Newspaper readers often write in to say they have seen road signs saying 'Cats' eyes removed'. But W. M. Richards, of Wimborne, Dorset, spotted that Dorset County Council had erected such a sign next to one advertising a veterinary clinic.

Daily Mail

Sign in Abbey Park in Evesham, Worcestershire: 'Decision time: toilets 75yds or 750yds.'

Spotted by Mrs Sue Tod, of Carlisle, *Daily Mail*

Classified ads in the *Rotherham Record*:
'Great Dame Puppies'
'Singing sewing machine'

Spotted by Hazel V. Green, Rotherham, South Yorkshire, *Daily Mail*

The Times carried a story about how theatres make highly critical judgements of their productions read like praise. Reader Brian Brooke-Smith, of Saffron Walden, Essex, recalled this phrase from a damning review in the newspaper: 'If your last train goes before the end, don't miss it.' 'Predictably,' writes Mr Brooke-Smith, 'the last three words were prominently displayed outside the theatre.'

The Times

Raffles Hotel in Singapore has a museum. One of the exhibits is a card with this quote from Kipling's *From Sea to Sea*: 'A place called Raffles Hotel, where the food is as excellent as the rooms.' But in a copy of *From Sea to Sea*, which is also displayed, the original quote reads: 'Raffles Hotel where the food is as excellent as the rooms are bad.'

Peter Cameron, Strathay, Perthshire, *The Times*

Newspapers cannot resist an excuse to scour through British place names looking for funny or naughty ones. After reports of Prince Harry renting a love nest in a Dorset hamlet named Shaggs, the *Sun* produced a list which included:
- Twatt – One in Orkney, one in Shetland
- Scratchy Bottom – Dorset
- Sandy Balls – Hampshire
- Brown Willy – Cornwall
- Titsey – Surrey

- Muff – County Donegal, which is reported to have a diving club
- Wyre Piddle – Worcestershire
- Prickwillow – Cambridgeshire.
- Aberllynfi Three Cocks – Powys

Sun

In August 2006 the *Guardian Diary* promised it would not print any more rude town names. But so many readers wrote in with their offerings that it was tempted to mention Gobblecock Hall in Suffolk and Shitterton in Devon.

Guardian

Sign at the Red Squirrel Reserve at Formby, near Southport: 'Squirrel food 30p. Please note: squirrel food contains nuts'
Spotted by David M. Clark, of Clapham Manchester,
Daily Mail

When John Henley's *Guardian Diary* happened to mention a sign which read, 'Squirrels drive carefully,' it unleashed 'a veritable torrent of side-splitting signs':
- This door is alarmed
- Dead slow children
- Chickens keep dogs on leads
- Humped zebra crossing
- Live on plasma
- Beware: heavy plant crossing

7

- This sign is not in use [*on the M2*]
- Train drivers must not be disturbed
- Button may be depressed [*on a food jar*]
- Leather faced manager's chair
- Parents with two or more children will have one Child to eat free [*in an Indian restaurant*]

A *Daily Mail* reader got in on the game with:

- Horses! Please close the gate

Guardian/Daily Mail

Sign in a Cornish fish and chip shop: 'Switch off your mobile or we will batter and fry it.'

Nigel Farndale, *Sunday Telegraph*

An advert for a farm attraction boasted: 'Traditional farmyard. Newborn lambs, chickens, ducks and geese. In Cuddle Corner: baby rabbits and guinea pigs, sheep, goats, calves, piglets, peacocks and game birds. New butcher's shop now open.'

Spotted by Mrs Christine McLanaghan of Canterbury, *Kentish Gazette*

Two signs seen in Peterborough:
'Beware: sleeping policeman. 10mph max'
Beneath this was a smaller sign saying:
'Quiet please'

John Barnes of Peterborough, *Daily Mail*

'Doesn't say much for the chef.' says the caption under a photograph of this sign outside a restaurant kitchen door in Camberwell, South-East London: 'No parking. Fire exit in constant use.'

Spotted by C. Broad, *Daily Mail*

People attending the Three Counties Show at Malvern were puzzled by a notice next to the Dog Show Entrance sign which read: 'No dogs beyond this point.'

Spotted by Pete Mitchell, Churchdown, Gloucestershire,
Daily Mail

Spotted at a harbour café on the Scottish coast by Rona Knox of Inverness: 'Wanted: odd job man to wash dishes and two waitresses.' 'Nice work if you can get it,' responded the *Daily Mail* headline.

Daily Mail

Notice at the entrance to Abberley Hall public school spotted by Christine Howells, of Cleobury Mortimer, Worcestershire: 'Please ensure gates are closed when entering or departing.'

Daily Mail

According to *Travel Trade Gazette* there's a Thai hotel which cautions guests: 'Do not bring solicitors into your room.'

Independent

Beneath the Fire Exit sign at a restaurant in St Ives, Cornwall, there is another sign saying 'Staff Only'.

A. O. Wilkinson, of Nottingham, *Daily Mail*

Sign spotted by *Daily Mail* reader D. Smith of Chelmsford, Essex at the Wickford branch of Aldi: 'Welcome to Aldi. Wheel clamping in operation. Aldi customers only.'

Daily Mail

Local sign seen by Mr Wood of Ipswich: 'Inniss Solicitors. Specialists in crime.'

Daily Mail

A sign at the Ashford Baby Warehouse proudly proclaimed: 'Save up to 60 per cent on end-of-line models.'

Maidstone Adscene

Seen outside Cromer High School by John Wilkinson of Kidderminster, Worcester – a bicycle leaning against a sign reading: 'Reserved emergency vehicle'.

Daily Mail

'If car park full please park elsewhere' – sign outside doctor's surgery.

Spotted by Miss B. Wilkinson of Knutsford, Cheshire, *Daily Mail*

A sign in a Norwich department store had an arrow pointing to the toilets. Immediately underneath it was another arrow pointing to The Place to Eat.

Spotted by Jack and Sheila Smart, *Daily Mail*

Spotted in a herbs and acupuncture shop by Paul Mogford, of Tiverton, Devon:
Special Offer
Hair Loss
15 per cent off

Daily Mail

Spotted on eBay by Ronald Sprason, of Markfield, Leicestershire: 'Every vehicle is serviced and valeted by our medicated staff.'

Daily Mail

In St Mawes, Cornwall, Mrs Mavis French, of Blackburn, Lancashire, came across a Shell petrol pump with a sign on it saying 2/3d a gallon. She says it is a pity that they turned up too late – the sign also said: 'Sorry. Sold out'.

Daily Mail

Spotted in Hemel Hempstead by Mrs P. M. Bassett, of Watford, Hertfordshire, a sign saying:
Doolittle Meadows

Business Park, *Daily Mail*

Tina, a three-legged tortoise, has been given a licence to roam off-road after having a pneumatic wheel with spring suspension and shock absorber system fitted. Darren Beasley, Tina's keeper at Longleat Safari Park in Wiltshire, says: 'She is able to get about all over the place. She is one of our oldest tortoises but you would never know it – she is now among our fastest.'

The Times

Chapter 2

SPORTING LIFE

M. F. Horton, of Alice Springs, Australia, tells the 1930s cricket story about England captain Douglas Jardine going to the Australians' dressing room demanding to know who had called him a bastard on the field. Australia's Viv Richardson is said to have called over to his team-mates: 'This bastard wants to know which of you bastards called him a bastard.'

The Times

A TV darts commentator told Simon Hoggart that the only people at darts matches who weren't drunk were the commentators. He recalled one top player being so drunk that when his opponent held out his hand in greeting he missed it.

Guardian

There was bitter criticism of a streaker at the 2006 Wimbledon championships. *Guardian* reader Martin Dibley, of Shanklin, Isle of Wight, commented: 'Imagine my horror – black socks on Centre Court!'

Guardian

A man was stopped on the London Underground for being in possession of a cricket ball. Iain Fenton, from Clackmannanshire (presumably a Scot), wrote: 'Surely if the ball was in the possession of an Englishman it could have presented little threat to anyone.'

Guardian

Manchester United star Wayne Rooney spotted a text message received by his girlfriend Coleen McLoughlin.
  'Who's this "Sam"?' demanded Wayne.
  'What are you on about?' responded Coleen
  'Who's Sam?' repeated the soccer star.
Coleen checked out the offending text message. 'Sam' turned out to be '5AM' – the time the message was sent.

Reported interview with Coleen in *Marie Claire* magazine, headed, 'Lovers' Tiff of the Week',
Sunday Times

John Hall, of Stamford, Lincolnshire, wonders if male football stars should copy their female counterparts. He watched the FA Women's Cup

Final in 2006 'and no scorer bared her midriff or took off her shirt in celebration.'

Daily Telegraph

Advice to fans on a Queen's Park Rangers match programme: 'Stay behind until the crowd has gone.'

Sunday Telegraph

World Cup football fever began to get well under way early in 2006. Superdrug stores did their bit selling condoms featuring a St George's Cross design on the pack along with the message 'Lie back and think of England'. The Sun's patriotic headline on this story was: 'England Going All The Way'.

Sun

A fish and chip shop owner near Leeds United's football ground had to throw away his stock of red plastic forks because they reminded local fans of their hated rivals – Manchester United.

Yorkshire Evening Post

In the days when cricket staged games between Gentlemen (amateurs) v. Players (professionals), the Gentlemen had separate dressing rooms and were called Mr – both in the scorebooks and by the Players. The Gentlemen's initials came before their names and the Professionals' initials came after.

This accounts for the infamous incident at Lord's

in the 1950s when Fred Titmus came out to bat. The announcer felt obliged to correct a scorecard error as follows:

Delete F. J. Titmus

Insert Titmus F. J.

New Statesman

Chris Connolly, of Chesterfield, Derbyshire, finds it marvellous to see the survival of the old tradition of county cricketers having wacky names:

- **Virgin, bowled Crump**
- **J. W. M. Dalrymple, c Mustard, b Onions**

Guardian

'The batsman's Holding, the bowler's Willey.'

BBC commentator Brian Johnston at the Oval Test match in 1976

David Joss Buckley of London nominates the most satisfying cricket score-book entry: 'Lillee, caught Willey, bowled Dilley.'

Guardian

The following explanation of cricket is not likely to throw much light on the game for newcomers, but it often appears in newspapers and magazines – and can be bought on a tea towel sold at Lord's:

- You have two sides, one out in the field and one in.

- Each player in the side that's in goes out and when he's out he goes in and the next player goes in until he's out.
- When all the players are out then the side that's out goes in and the side that's in goes out and tries to get those coming in out.
- Sometimes you get players still in and not out.
- When both sides have been in and out, including the not outs, that's the end of the game.

> Lord's souvenir tea towel and various
> newspapers and magazines

After being appointed captain of the England cricket team, Andrew Flintoff recalled some of the highlights of his career, and said: 'When I was 17 I got hit in the knackers batting. I put them in iced water and then put the glass on one side. Gary Yates, the Lancashire spinner, came in from training and drank the water.'

Observer Magazine

Fred Trueman died on 1 July 2006, aged 75. The Yorkshire star was one of the greatest fast bowlers of all time – and renowned for his ripe and stormy personality. Every newspaper carried obits full of Truemanisms (claiming many of them to be true):

- Anything suggestive of a Harlequin cap was anathema to him. He watched with ill-concealed disgust as one such exquisite made his way to the middle at Lord's, complete with matching cravat. The dandy's stumps were immediately shattered and as the hapless batsman returned to the pavilion Fiery Fred observed: "Ardly worth getting dressed up for, were it?'

- On the tour of Australia in 1962–63, the Reverend David Sheppard dropped several catches. Trueman advised him: 'Kid yourself it's Sunday, Rev – and keep your hands together.'

- It was the unshakable belief in his own ability which made him the bowler he was – and the conviction that there were two ways of doing things: his way and the wrong way.

- To a batsman coming out of the pavilion: 'Don't bother closing t'gate. Tha'll not be out here long.'

- To a University batsman who congratulated Fred after being out first ball. 'Aye, but bloody wasted on thee.'

Numerous papers

Brenda Rose has happy memories sitting as a lay magistrate along with a judge at Westminster Crown Court. They were hearing a complicated case when an usher handed a note to the judge and a respectful silence fell on the court while he read it.

'After a moment he passed the note to me: "Australia all out for 312."'

The Times, under the heading: 'Silence in Court'

English football fans eager to visit Germany for the 2006 World Cup were offered a specially tailored language course at the Joseph Priestley College in Leeds, which taught them the German for 'Have you seen my lucky Union Jack underpants? (Hast du mein tolle Unterhose gesehen?)

The Times

An all-women skittles team in Gloucester was told to move out by their club because its members did not drink enough. The ladies were told that when they played the club bar made only £20-£30 a night. When male teams played the bar made £120.

A club official said: 'We've got to keep afloat.'

Daily Telegraph and other papers

English football clubs spend millions hiring foreign players. This upsets traditional fans – as demonstrated by the letter from Bob Bury, of Leeds; when Arsenal lost to Barcelona in the Champions League final in May 2006: 'Just imagine how much worse we would feel if an English team had been involved.'

The Times

For those of its readers who couldn't bear the thought of 5,670 minutes of World Cup football on the TV, *The Times* produced a list of alternatives. They included:

- Live like a footballer's wife at the Premiership's favourite Welsh hotel.
- Stay at Linthwaite House Hotel in Bowness, Cumbria, which has forbidden staff to mention the F word.
- Attend Ladies Day at Royal Ascot.
- Visit the World Nettle Eating Championships at the Bottle Inn, Marshwood, Dorset.
- Attend the World Pea Shooting Championships at Witcham, Cambridgeshire.

The Times

Capital Radio presenter Johnny Vaughan listed some of the suggestions following a request for ideas for a collective noun for footballers' wives:

- A giggle
- A meow
- A vacuum
- A sashay
- A shallow
- A vulgarity
- An excess
- A cleavage

Daily Telegraph

Amid a flood of stories about Scots cheering for teams opposing England in the World Cup, Sally Parker, of Poole, Dorset, reported seeing a West Highland terrier with a red cross sprayed on its back: 'Could there be any greater indignity to a dog of Scottish descent?'

Daily Telegraph

Tory MP Sir Malcolm Rifkind claims he is the only man ever to unite the fans of Glasgow's Celtic and Rangers football teams. When he was Scottish Secretary he banned alcohol at a match between the two rivals. He attended the match – and both sets of fans booed him.

Sun

Two English World Cup fans took a careful note of where they had parked their car in Cologne – but still could not find it after the game. So they approached a German policeman and showed him the street name they had written down: 'Einbahn Strasse' – 'One-way Street'.

Sunday Times

David Powell, of Lewes, East Sussex, writes: 'Having nominally "invented" rugby, cricket, tennis and soccer, isn't it time England invented a game it can win?'

Guardian

While others at the World Cup were trying their best not to mention the war, the *Guardian* reported that in Nuremburg the England Supporters' Band '...gave a spirited rendition of the theme from that great 1954 contribution to Anglo-German relations – The Dambusters'.

Meanwhile the *The Times* called attention to the number of blogs devoted to cats that look like Hitler.

Guardian/The Times

There were tears all round when England were penalty-kicked out of the World Cup, but *The Times* kept a stiff upper lip with 'Now Its All Over – 11 Reasons To Be Cheerful'. Among the reasons:

- We've got two years to practice penalty kicks before Euro 2008.
- You can have a normal conversation with your spouse again
- The WAGS (the shopaholic wives and girlfriends of English players) will return to relative obscurity.
- That's enough Rooney. No longer do we have to regard this cross between Shrek and a Bash Street Kid as the cream of English manhood.

The Times

When Prince William arrived at RAF Lyneham, Wiltshire, to fly to the World Cup, his driver missed the VIP entrance and pulled up at the main gate. The young

22

airman on guard asked for William's ID and, upon perusing it, said: 'Oh f***, it's you innit?'

William replied: I'm afraid so, can I come in?'

What a refreshing lack of 'Don't you know who I am?' reported the *Sun's* 'The Whip' column.

Sun

As England plunged out of the World Cup in 2006 cartoonist Matt produced one of the brilliant page one cartoons that make him a regular award winner. Immigrants are seen leaving a Britishness Class and telling a friend: 'Today we learned how to miss a penalty.'

Daily Telegraph

Within days of England being kicked out of the World Cup the price of England flags fell from £1 to 1p.

The Times

A Yorkshire village cricket team got a place in the record books when all of its batsmen were out for a duck. Goldsborugh's second team – struggling at the bottom of the fourth division in the North Yorkshire Nidderdale League – knew they were in for a tough match against league leaders Dishforth. But they were skittled out for a total of five – four byes and a leg-bye. Dishforth went in and scored the necessary six runs for victory and the game was over in 60 minutes.

Peter Horsman, rueful captain of Goldsborough, said: 'It was both surreal and embarrassing... but it still beats shopping on a Saturday.'

Goldsborough's No.11, John Tomkinson, was reported by *The Times* to 'have carried his bat for an heroic, unbeaten 0'. John posted this message on the club's website: 'So it's not my fault then.'

Yorkshire Post/The Times/Sun

The Nidderdale Amateur League cricket team that was all out for ten ducks were admired for how well they took their humiliation after the captain said he hoped the experience would be character-building for his players.

Sunday Telegraph

The lowest innings score in a Test match was New Zealand's 26 against England at Auckland in 1955. England's lowest Test score was 45 against Australia at Sydney in 1886-87.

The Times, under the very English headline: 'It's Not the Winning that Matters'.

A *Sunday Telegraph* writer was invited to play for his village side in Suffolk and was told of a local rule that you cannot be out first ball. He recalled another team with the quirky rule that everyone had to bowl.

Another had a bearded professor smoking a pipe at deep square leg. Silly mid off was an old lady, one of

the bowlers was a 12-year-old boy, and the pavilion clock went backwards.

'This is the beguiling thing about amateur cricket. You can more or less make it up as you go along', writes Nigel Farndale.

Sunday Telegraph

The original Wembley Stadium was built in 1923 at a cost of £750,000 and was completed in 300 days – well within schedule. Today, that £750,000 would have the spending power of £28.5million.

In August 2006, the cost of the new Stadium was estimated at £757million.

Daily Express

As the 2006–07 Ashes series approached, Australian cricket fans were asked to perform what the *Daily Telegraph* called 'an apparently impossible task of mental gymnastics.'

Cricket Australia, the game's governing body in Oz, ruled that English fans can be called 'Poms' or 'Pommies' – but warned that fans from Down Under must avoid linking the P-word with anything 'hurtful... racist, offensive or humiliating'.

It was a Page One story for the *Telegraph*, which said that the last time an Englishman at a match in Australia was called a 'Pom' without an offensive epithet 'is lost in the mists of time'.

On its leader page the *Telegraph* said that the word

Pom, shorn of any antipodean qualifier, is a feeble thing. It thought England's Barmy Army tough enough to endure the 'fecund repository of invective that is the Australian fan. Let's face it – if we retain the Ashes, we won't give a XXXX what they call us.'

Daily Telegraph

Britain's biggest bus company First Group employs 1,000 Polish drivers and has set up a training base in Lublin, south-east Poland. Trainees take a course in dialects with *Only Fools and Horses* being shown to those destined to drive in London and Billy Connolly concerts for those going to Glasgow. *The Stoke Sentinel* was the set text for two drivers posted to the Potteries.

Guardian

Old Moore and his Almanack, who have been forecasting the future for some 310 years, said the 2007 Derby would be won by the second favourite. Another forecast for 2007 looked like being a safer bet:

'MAY – Saturn's continued opposition to Neptune points to ongoing government muddle and the chance that most initiatives will fail.'

Independent Magazine

England's cricketing disasters in Australia in 2006–07 gave us yet another chance to prove what wonderful losers we are. Mr A. Moore, of Droxford,

Hampshire, got us off to a good start by sending this item to the *Daily Mail*:

'The Seven Dwarfs were busy in their mine when the roof caved in. Snow White could find no trace of them and yelled tearfully: "Can anyone hear me?"

A voice floated up from the bowels of the mine: "England might beat Australia next time."

"Thank goodness," said Snow White. "At least Dopey's still alive."'

Daily Mail

Gerry Smith, of London, wrote to the *Daily Telegraph*, saying that following England's abysmal performance the MBEs should be handed back and the team should turn to Strictly Come Dancing:

'In the light of the dancing success of Darren Gough and Mark Ramprakash, this is the only successful career path for English cricketers at the present time.'

Daily Telegraph

Leo McKinstry of the *Sunday Telegraph* wrote: 'As England return from Australia in sackcloth but without the Ashes, the wholesale award of medals looks more farcical than ever.'

Geoff Boycott, whose batting used to display exactly the kind of toughness that England lacked, said that he was so fed up that he had decided to give his own OBE (awarded in the 1970s) to his cat.

Sunday Telegraph

David Fine went to Australia as the England team's poet in residence. But the team's performance became an artistic problem at times. 'I mean,' he said, 'how many ways can you spell "lament"?'

Before packing his bags for the sad journey home, Fine was reported to be still looking for a rhyme for whitewash.

Observer

In a spirit of true British grit, the *Daily Telegraph* bravely penned the following rhyme:

Oh how the English revel in defeat
Even when the whitewash is so complete.

Daily Telegraph

Are we down at what happened down under? Not a bit of it. The Barmy Army wasn't crushed – though many of them had spent £8,ooo on the trip, their chants could be heard around the Sydney ground long after the final humiliating ball.

'The more we lose the more we sing,' roared David Grimes, 27, a Barmy Army stalwart from Lincoln.

Vic Flowers, 54, from Oldham, regarded as the Army's unofficial leader, uttered words every bit as stirring as those Shakespeare attributed to Henry V on St Crispin's Eve.

'We'll reclaim what's rightly ours in two years time,' he said with complete conviction.

Daily Telegraph

Inevitably, cruel jokes about England's cricketing performance were soon flying around the Internet:

*Why didn't the England fielders need
travel injections?*
Because they never catch anything.

*Why did England players demand increased
match payments?*
Someone told them that Ashes Tests
sometimes go to a fourth day.

*What do you call an English cricketer with
100 runs against his name?*
A bowler.

How bad was the English batting?
The selectors are thinking of moving Extras up
the batting order.

Daily Telegraph

For some it sounded like the end of civilisation as we know it. The *Daily Telegraph* reported on 12 January 2007 that Ascot was going to let punters buy their way into the Royal Enclosure – 'in one of the greatest breaks with tradition since the ban on divorcees was lifted in 1955'.

Although undischarged bankrupts are still unwelcome, and admission of ex-prisoners is at the discretion of officials, the decision to grant entry as part of fine dining packages has outraged some racegoers.

Enclosure passes are included as an inducement to buy lunch at prices from £530 to £1,410 per person. Coach parties are welcome – but they must abide by the dress code. (Top hats and morning suits for men. Women to wear hats and not expose their midriffs.

The Royal Enclosure was established in the 1790s. Entrance was strictly by invitation from George III himself.

An un-named Ascot regular harrumphed: 'We have gone from the sport of kings to the sport of chavs.'

Daily Telegraph

A poll of around 650 sportsmen and women revealed that almost four in five of them have superstitious rituals.

- David Coulthard wore the underpants he had on when he won his first Grand Prix until they wore out.
- David Beckham touches the grass in the centre circle before the kick-off.
- Former England scrum half Austin Healey sought out cinemas to buy popcorn before a game. 'I had to buy popcorn and eat it. No one else was allowed to eat my popcorn.'
- Tiger Woods believes that a red shirt makes him more likely to win.

Daily Mail

Horse racing's board of censors scrutinises the names of 15,000 thoroughbreds a year and weeds out the ridiculous, the naughty and the downright obscene. A constant desire to hoodwink the system has led the board to compile a table of names that failed in 2006.

Welsh-sounding 'Llamedos' and 'Llareggubb' are frequently tried and always rejected for what they spell backwards. Among the top naughtiest names rejected in 2006 were:

- Betty Swallocks
- Drew Peacock
- Far Kinnel
- Noble Ox
- Wear the Fox Hat
- Some slip through the censor – Who Gives a Donald being one of them.

Daily Telegraph

It is said to be an old tradition down at Chelsea Football Club's Stamford Bridge ground. The fans there are reported to be addicted to throwing sticks of celery.

But grumpy club officials take a dim view and have issued this warning: 'The throwing of anything at a football match, including celery, is a criminal offence for which you can be arrested and end up with a criminal record.'

Guardian

'What wonderful English sportsmanship,' we all said when TV showed Freddie Flintoff apparently consoling Australian bowler Brett Lee immediately after England's epic victory in the second game of the 2005 Ashes.

But... Freddie's friend Rory Bremner says that when a fan asked Flintoff what he said to Lee, Freddie replied: 'I said, "It's 1-1 you Aussie bastard!"'

Daily Mail

Chapter 3

LAW AND DISORDER

After a man stole £300 worth of skin products from Superdrug in Egham, police issued this description of him: 'White, in his 20s, 5ft 9in tall and spotty'.

Guardian

Immigration officials turned down an applicant for a visa because they did not believe he wanted to spend a week's holiday in Gateshead.

Sunday Telegraph

Travellers who posed as tree surgeons to swindle money out of elderly customers were caught after offering to prune a poplar tree which was, in fact, an ivy-clad telegraph pole.

Winchester Crown Court, Hampshire, remanded them in custody and warned that they faced jail.

Daily Telegraph

Muggers in Margate have snatched 71-year-old Martha Reed's bag three times, not realising that she carries it only to scoop up her dog's poo.

Sun

Community Support officers in the West Midlands reprimanded two children for playing hopscotch. The children were made to scrub off the hopscotch grids they had chalked on the pavement – a punishment designed 'to prevent them sliding into more serious crime'.

Daily Mirror/Independent on Sunday

Spotted in a Southend paper by Les Gibson of Leigh-on-Sea, Essex: 'Thieves broke into a van in Benfleet and stole a microscope worth £1,500. Police are looking into it.'

Daily Mail

A man who called a police surgeon a 'f***ing Paki' was advised by an Exeter Crown Court judge: 'Next time call him a fat bastard and don't say anything about his colour.'

The Times

The Home Office allowed the Duchess of Northumberland to grow six cannabis plants as part of an educational display at Alnwick Garden, Northumberland.

They were stolen by someone not believed to be deeply involved in education.

The Times

After Laura Partington, 23, battered a burglar with a saucepan in her flat in Gloucester, Judge Jamie Tabor told her that it was a matter of public regret that she did not hit him harder. This, despite the fact that the pan broke during the altercation.

The Times/Daily Telegraph

An 18-year-old convicted burglar escaped from a hospital bed and ended up begging a judge at Cardiff Crown Court to send him back to prison 'because I will never finish my A-level exams on the outside'.

Sentenced to an extra year for escaping he called out, 'Thanks.'

Sunday Times

Thieves who robbed a van on its way to Heathrow got away with £75million – in Monopoly money. Police vowed to nab the bungling bandits and bang them up 'with no Get Out of Jail Free card'.

Sun

Devon and Cornwall police have received thousands of 'inappropriate' 999 calls including:

- One from a drunk who wanted to be driven home.
- Another reporting a pigeon in distress.
- One asking for them to deliver a pizza.

Cornish Times

Seen scrawled in the grime on the doors of a security van carrying prisoners through Kilmarnock, Scotland: 'Toot if they jump oot.'

Guardian

Police in Lancashire, West Sussex and Herefordshire have separately been on race-crime raids to toy shops with golliwogs on display.

Daily Mail

What are we talking about in the items below:
- **A 1 in 14 chance of being walloped on the head?**
- **A 1 in 50 chance of being fatally wounded in an attack?**
- **A 4 to 5 per cent chance of copping a depressed fracture of the skull?**
- **A danger of having your ears cut off, although blunt instruments are usually the weapons of choice?**

Forget about yobbo Asbo candidates rampaging in the streets of our cities. This was all going on in 'the

crime-ridden Stone Age, when it was hardly safe to leave your cave.'

The statistics were divined by experts examining hundreds of skulls from Southern England – believed to date from 4,000 to 3,200 BC

Daily Mail

Jurors are more likely to convict defendants who are ugly, say psychologists from Bath Spa University.

Daily Telegraph

In the spring of 2006 there was a water shortage in parts of Britain and a ban on the use of hosepipes was imposed. People were urged to snitch on any neighbours seen ignoring the ban.

Stephen Glover in the *Daily Mail* wrote that acting as a 'copper's nark' was 'deeply unBritish' – and revealed that it is estimated that there are more than 100 hotlines which 'narks' can ring to shop their fellow citizens.

They include snitchers' numbers for reporting people painting graffiti, abandoning vehicles and being rowdy.

Daily Mail

Criminals impersonating staff at the Department of Work and Pensions were believed to have swiped around £30 million.

Ephraim Hardcastle's gossip column in the *Daily Mail*'s reported: 'I am informed that the thieves were particularly enterprising – they appropriated the identities of members of the department's fraud squad.'

Daily Mail/Computerworld

A dispute over a 10p unpaid parking fee has cost Kirklees Council more than £2,500 in legal costs. On 25 April 2006, Nick Newby, 45, of Gomersal, near Bradford, attended his sixth court hearing when Leeds Crown Court was told that the car park involved in the dispute was now a free car park.

Judge Rodney Grant said he was 'speechless' and the case was adjourned.

The Times

In April 2006 District Judge Jonathan Finestein condemned a decision to bring a 10-year-old boy to court for calling one of his schoolmates 'Bin Laden' and 'Paki'. Greater Manchester Police had charged the boy with a 'racially aggravated public order offence', but the judge condemned it all as 'political correctness gone mad'.

The Crown Prosecution Service finally decided not to go ahead and the Muslim Council of Great Britain welcomed the decision. 'A victory for common sense,' said some.

The accused 10-year-old told the court that the other boy had called him 'white trash', but the two of them were now good friends.

Daily Mail/Guardian/Press Association/The Times

Thieves used an oxyacetylene torch to break into a hole-in-the-wall machine in Calcot, Berkshire – but ran off empty-handed when the money burst into flames.

Metro

Brian Winkworth, of Waterlooville, Hampshire, noted the following national differences:
- In Britain everything is permitted, except that forbidden by law.
- In Germany, everything is forbidden, except that permitted by law.
- In the Soviet Union everything is forbidden, including that permitted by law.
- In Italy, everything is permitted, including that forbidden by law.

The Times

Reading Crown Court heard how James Robin had stolen a bike to make sure he was not late for a hearing at a magistrate's court where he was appearing on a burglary charge.

Guardian

Surrey police are writing to householders asking them to indicate 'identifiable hazards' in their homes should a police officer need to attend. The list of possible hazards includes slippery floors, ceiling beams, ponds, basements, and sprinkler systems.

Daily Telegraph

Douglas Dick, a former chemical engineer and railway enthusiast, found a way round hosepipe bans during the 2006 drought. He laid a five-inch gauge railway track around his garden in Shepperton, Surrey, fitted one of his eight rainwater butts onto a bogie and attached a boat pump to a 12-volt battery.

All that he and his wife Sally had to do was push the 'tank wagon' to where it was needed and water away gleefully and legally.

Daily Telegraph

An Asbo was served on Paul Henney, 44, stopping him slamming the doors in his flat in Great Yarmouth.

Daily Telegraph

Warders found that inmates playing with tennis balls in Kingston Prison, Portsmouth, were not developing an interest in the game as Wimbledon 2006 approached.

It was discovered that the balls had been hit over the prison walls by friends of the prisoners – and were stuffed with cannabis.

Daily Telegraph

Police have devised a cunning plan to thwart bicycle thieves in Cheltenham. They have adapted some bikes so that they cannot be pedalled at fast speeds. The go-slow bikes are then left unattended with officers skulking nearby, out of sight, ready to pounce.

Said one officer: 'Thieves are more likely to be caught now we are using these sting bikes.'

Guardian

David Harris, of Corbridge, Northumberland, appealed against a £60 speeding ticket – and ended up with a £4,500 bill after police flew in an expert witness from America.

David questioned the accuracy of a mobile speed gun which had clocked him as doing 90mph. So police brought in the boss of the US firm which supplies the guns, and Hexham magistrates ruled that Dick must pay the cost of bringing the expert over.

Sun

Two armed robbers raided Edenfield Post Office in Lancashire and ordered the postmaster to fill up a bag with money. They ran off with a pack of strawberries after picking up the wrong bag.

The Times

In one of the latest attempt to evade Scotland's strict ban on public smoking, a man was spotted in the Firth of Forth in a child's inflatable rubber ring smoking a cigar.

When approached by HM Coast Guards, he said he was fine and did not require any assistance.

Edinburgh Evening News

A 28-year-old man from High Wycombe was fined £1,000 for selling a spray to prevent speed cameras reading number plates – because it didn't work.

The Times

A 72-year-old pensioner involved in a boundary dispute was jailed for a day by Grantham magistrates after pleading guilty to repeatedly urinating on his neighbour's fast-growing leylandii trees.

There are thought to be some 17,000 leylandii wars going on in the UK.

The Times

In August 2006 Kent police reported that some 60 items had been stolen from them in the past year. These included a mountain bike, forensic science equipment, handcuffs, number plates from a patrol car, a police helmet – and a cap from an officer's head in Thanet.

Daily Telegraph

Computer expert John Ellison installed a £20,000 security system with 16 CCTV cameras at his home in Lancaster and then went on holiday to Marbella.

When burglars broke into his house they triggered an alert which enabled Mr Ellison to see the raiders on his laptop. He dialled 999 and, from 1,600 miles away, was able to watch police arrive and cart off the villains in handcuffs.

He celebrated with a bottle of champagne and the burglars were convicted at Lancaster Magistrates' Court.

Daily Telegraph

Rod Liddle in the *Sunday Times* put up some strong possibles for a suggested Ludicrous Hate Crime Award wherein our constabularies vie for bringing the most stupid cases. Early contenders included:

- Metropolitan Police unsuccessfully prosecuted two Tube workers wrongly accused of biting off the heads of black jelly babies 'in a racially intimidating manner'.
- Central Scotland's aborted prosecution of a mechanic from Stirling for 'revving his car in a racist manner'.
- Thames Valley arrested a chap who suggested that a police horse might be 'gay' – thus 'causing offence and distress to a police officer and his horse'.

Sunday Times

The Lancashire constabulary sent three traffic cars and a dog patrol unit in pursuit of a vehicle. 'Stingers' were placed in the path of the offending vehicle – devices which should have blown out its tyres.

The miscreant, however, managed to evade the cunning trap – but the four chasing police vehicles did not and 'were immediately incapacitated'.

Police Magazine/Guardian

Bungling burglars and criminal crackpots:

- A 34-year-old burglar was enjoying the luxury of a hot bath when the houseowner returned and found him naked in the bath. The burglar got eight months.

- A 37-year-old thief was caught when his image was recorded by a CCTV camera he was stealing.

- A burglar was caught frying fish after the smell woke up the householder.

- A 37-year-old attempted to burgle the house of combative Everton footballer Duncan Ferguson and required two days of hospital treatment after Ferguson woke up during the raid.

- A 28-year-old burglar from Wandsworth, London, was arrested after asking a policeman to help him carry stolen goods over a fence.

The Times

Sgt Tony Smith and PC Mike Holman dressed up as Batman and Robin and pretended they were looking for a fancy dress party. They knocked on a suspect's door and, after a chase, nicked him in Weymouth, Dorset.

Sgt Smith complained that his Batman outfit did not provide him with anywhere to hang his handcuffs.

Dorset Echo, under the headline: 'KA-POW!!! You're Nicked!!'

Some criminal crackpots were on the loose in 2006. A man who raided a hunting lodge in Lancashire, belonging to the Duke of Westminster, enjoyed the contents of the drinks cabinet. He got tipsy on fine claret and then decided to cook himself a meal. After he had drunkenly switched on the gas cooker there was an explosion which blew off part of the roof and he finished up among the wreckage with burns to face and hands. Firemen had to cut their way into the building to rescue him.

Police said later that the drinks cabinet was believed to have contained three bottles of claret and that the stricken intruder had 'consumed the lot'.

The Times

A dozy burglar was caught asleep in bed at a flat he had been ransacking in Cam, Gloucester.

Sun

A man was jailed for four months after being filmed by a CCTV camera he was stealing in Plymouth.

The Times

An elderly man came out of the post office at Bury St Edmonds. Three muggers approached him demanding 'Hand it over.' The OAP then laid out the ringleader with a left hook to the chin.

The pensioner just happened to be George Bayliss, former international boxer and Army middle-weight champion.

Independent on Sunday

A 22-year-old woman suspected of shoplifting was caught by security staff in Exeter. She tried to escape by slipping out of her jeans, revealing that she was wearing nothing underneath.

The bare-bottomed suspect was photographed by a witness who said: 'When she dropped her trousers we saw everything.'

The Times/Sun (with picture)

Hangman Albert Pierrepoint described John Amery, an aristocratic delinquent turned traitor, as 'the bravest man I ever hanged'.

Pierrepoint said that when he entered the condemned cell in Wandsworth Prison Amery said: 'I have always wanted to meet you, though not, of course, in these circumstances.'

Pierrepoint also said that 'execution could bring the best out of the worst people'.

Sunday Telegraph

Police Constable Mark White sounded a touch saddened in his letter to *The Times* after discovering that 'we no longer have snouts, grasses or informants'.

It seems PCs who want to be PC refer to 'Covert Human Intelligence Sources' instead.

The Times

The Times published a Cut Out and Keep Guide to the perfect EU banana published under the headline: 'Why is this banana legally curved instead of just crooked? Answer: Because it is the fruit of the finest judicial minds in Europe.'

Under EU Regulation 2257/94 bananas are required to be at least 5.5 inches long and 1.06 inches round and to not have 'abnormal curvature' – as set out in an eight-page directive.

The Times

Police suspected that Simon Hooper, 28, had stolen and swallowed a diamond engagement ring in a jeweller's shop in Dorchester. He denied it and was put in a cell to allow 'nature to take its course'.

Simon stuck it out and police had to seek an extension to the time they could hold him.

Three days and three nights later the £1,750 ring emerged. Police cleaned up the evidence and magistrates in Blandford, Dorset jailed Hooper for 12 weeks.

Guardian

As Government departments go, you'd imagine the Ministry of Defence might be one of the most secure. But in the last ten years twenty-nine of its works of art have been stolen and none of them recovered.

Daily Telegraph

The *Guardian Diary*'s 'Coveted Mastermind of the Month Award' went to Trevor Doyle, 25, in January 2007. After a weekend release, he fell asleep on the bus that was returning him to his open prison – so he stole a car to get him back in time for the deadline.

Guardian

Another possible contender for the Award could have been the 22-year-old who rang for a cab from his own home and then robbed the driver. He got three years at Portsmouth Crown Court.

The Times

A judge sitting at Minshull Street Crown Court, Manchester, decided that a policeman who gave two teenage tearaways a clip round the ear had 'acted in the best traditions of the force'.

Daily Telegraph

A Lincolnshire mother got an Asbo for singing Gary Glitter songs in the bath too loudly.

Independent on Sunday

Reading Crown Court was told that police caught a burglar after he dropped his mobile phone at the scene of the crime – the instrument contained his picture.

The burglar, from Slough in Berkshire, got 160 hours' community service.

Daily Telegraph

South Lanarkshire Council slapped an Asbo on a local woman – banning her from answering the door in her underwear.

Observer

Theatre director and amateur sculptor Sir Jonathan Miller offered a scrap dealer some bits hanging about in his garden (two halves of an old cast-iron bath). Later he discovered to his horror that the scrap merchant had also carted off three original Miller sculptures.

'They were some of the best pieces I've done,' he told his local paper ruefully.

Sunday Times

It was reported in April 2007 that new laws could mean imprisonment for people who allowed their pets to become too fat.

This caused Dr Donald Stevens to ponder if we would see Christopher Robin behind bars, and perhaps, Rabbit, too, for providing the wherewithal that caused Pooh to be stuck in the entrance to his rabbit-hole for a week.

Daily Telegraph

Police swooped on a five year-old boy after he chalked a hopscotch court on a pavement in a quiet cul-de-sac where he lives in Burnham-on-Sea, Somerset. The officers of the law were 'acting on a tip off' from a neighbour who thought the traditional British children's game involved creating graffiti on the pavement.

But it all turned out to be a bit of a wash-out because rain not only stopped play – it washed out the hopscotch court.

Western Morning News

Chapter 4

BEST OF BRITISHNESS

Most British toilets flush in the key of E flat.

Prospect Magazine

Are Cockneys funnier than Scousers? Can the Welsh make jokes as well as being the butt of them? The Open University hopes to find out with the aid of a travelling Joke Booth. In advance of the academic hunt for British humour, *The Times* gave these samples:

Best British Joke

A woman gets on a bus with her baby and the driver says: 'That's the ugliest baby I've ever seen.'

She says to the passenger sitting next to her: 'The driver just insulted me.'

The passenger says: 'You go tell him off. I'll hold your monkey.'

Top Joke in England

Two weasels are sitting in a bar and one says to the other: 'I slept with your mother!' The bar goes quiet as everyone waits to see how the other weasel will react.

The first weasel does it again, shouting this time: 'I SLEPT WITH YOUR MOTHER!'

The other weasel says: 'Go home Dad. You're drunk.'

The Times

Not everyone will celebrate the story published by the *Sunday Times* in May 2006, which asked: 'Could it be the end for a great British institution?' After studying 6,000 male bottoms in Britain and America, an underwear firm has invented a pair of boxer shorts that stretch like skin and can keep even the largest behind covered.

An irreverent spokesman said: 'This is officially the end of builders' bum'.

Sunday Times

Tim Arnold, of Slough, Buckinghamshire, wrote that on 9 February 2007 his *Daily Telegraph* failed to materialise in his letterbox because two inches snow had fallen.

'There can be no greater symbol of the decline of a once-great nation,' he concluded.

Daily Telegraph

A 2004 edition of a guidebook on Britain says that it is a country where everything stops for afternoon tea with scones and cucumber sandwiches. Everyone wears tweed and the trains run on time. The guide assures visitors that long periods of adverse weather are rare and the average rainfall is quite low.

Another guide notes that cultural eccentricities that set the British apart include queuing and warns visitors that pushing in is 'likely to cause an outburst of affronted tutting'.

The Times

Many Brits were dismayed that a US organisation wanted to teach American tourists not to appear arrogant, insensitive, over-materialistic and ignorant about local values when travelling abroad. Sam Leith in the *Daily Telegraph* says the organisation 'entirely misses the point that this is why we like them... Patronising American tourists is one of the few ways we have of bolstering our ridiculous sense of national pride.'

Daily Telegraph

A government plan to teach children the traditional values of Britishness got a rough going over by Guardian readers. Joe Phillips, 71, of Bingham, Nottinghamshire, writes: 'Reviewing the core values of my youth, I recall that every good Briton regarded all foreigners as inferior, smelly and thieves.'

Guardian

A Government-backed project to identify the great icons that help to define English identity has produced a list that includes:

- Big Ben
- Blackpool Tower
- Constable's 'The Hay Wain'
- Cricket
- A cup of tea
- FA Cup Final
- Hadrian's Wall
- The miniskirt
- Morris dancing
- The Notting Hill Carnival
- The pub
- Punch and Judy
- The Routemaster bus
- St George's flag
- The Spitfire
- Stonehenge
- York Minster

Daily Telegraph/Guardian/Daily Mail

At the end of its report on the 'English identity' project, *The Times* said that suggestions for icons that speak loudly of England but were unlikely to make the list included:

- An Asbo
- A hospital waiting list
- John Prescott
- An out-of-town Tesco

The Times

The next day *The Times* returned to the icons subject and, under the headline 'Reasons to be Proud', reported on 'Why England is great' according to the Culture Department's icons project: 'Who else boasts eggy soldiers, the misplaced apostrophe and Shakespeare's plays.'

The Times

Celebrities came forward with their ideas and actor Bob Hoskins suggested 'The achievements of Dame Judy Dench'. Fashion designer Mary Quant proposed cardigans and cottage pie.

Daily Telegraph

What snobs the British are. They lie, lie and lie again about where they live, according to a Norwich Union Direct survey called 'Power of the Postcode' published in May 2006. More than half are prepared to fib about their address to appear more 'upmarket'.

In West London many who live in Acton pretend to live in Chiswick. People in the hideous hinterland of the Harrow Road say they live in leafy Maida Vale. There are those who have pretensions to residing in desirable W11 (Notting Hill), when in reality they live in the less salubrious W12 (Shepherd's Bush).

The survey uncovered examples all over the country of residents 'adopting' more exclusive-sounding addresses.

There is an estate agent's tale of one buyer who would not move to East Bergholt, which has an Essex code although it is in Suffolk, because he did not want his daughter to be an Essex girl.

Examples of where people actually live and where they say they live include:

- Scunthorpe = 'North Lincolnshire'
- Hull = 'Cottingham'
- Oldham = 'Saddleworth'
- West Norwood = 'Dulwich Village'
- Birmingham = 'Solihill'
- Brighton = 'Hove'
- Slough = 'Windsor/Maidenhead'

Daily Telegraph/Daily Mail

The famous 1973 Hovis bread advert – showing a little boy pushing his delivery bike up a steep, cobbled village – hill was voted Britain's favourite advertisement in 2006.

Andrew O'Hagan writes that the sepia advert's

account of English decency '... plays on romantic images of English endurance and pride: the brass band, the cloth cap, the row of modest houses and the coveted bicycle'. It offers a notion of a simpler, more basic way of life, a fundamental Britishness... a place of warm beer and cricket on the village green.

'Nostalgia has long since become an industry in itself, and one that the British do better than most.'

Daily Telegraph

Gloom descended upon Britain when it was announced that the manufacture of HP sauce – a staple of British tables for more than 100 years – was to be moved to Holland. It was little comfort to learn that the iconic delicacy would still carry a picture of the Houses of Parliament on its label.

The Times filled page eight with the shock news and told of the days when Prime Minister Harold Wilson used the sauce so much that it was known as Wilson's Gravy.

The *Daily Telegraph* had a page one story headlined: 'British are browned off as HP Sauce goes Dutch'.

Times/Daily Telegraph

Time Out magazine published a list of 101 things about London 'that make us chuckle, guffaw and laugh-out loud. They included:

- Saveloys – a melange of gristle and eyeballs in

a pink casing that remains inexplicably popular in the world's food capital

- The claim that London is the world's food capital
- The rumour that Sir Norman Foster had the idea for the Gherkin when he was in the bath.
- People pretending to drive the Docklands Light Railway.
- Cockfosters, Cock Hill, Cock Lane, Back Passage, Pratts Walk, Horniman, Ass House Lane.
- The hairdressers in Bethnal Green called 'It'll Grow Back'.

Time Out

When Central European filmmaker Alexander Korda was made a British subject in 1936 he celebrated with this toast: 'Down with bloody foreigners.'

Daily Mail

Jeff Randall in the *Daily Telegraph*'s business section opined that the British remain world leaders at making up excuses. He set up a competition and among the excuses submitted by his readers were:

- Some of my chickens were in the driveway with their feet frozen in the snow. I just couldn't drive over them.

The wife of a senior clerk explained that her

husband was off work 'with a heavy cold and a slight touch of syphilis.'

- A Somerset woman said she had to drive her children to the village school each day because letting them walk there was too dangerous. 'Too many cars on the road,' she explained.

Daily Telegraph

In 1946 England's footballers won the World Cup – and Barclays Bank launched Britain's first credit card. In the forty years that followed English football has not blossomed but Britain has become credit-crazy and is the only country in Europe with more credit cards than people. This despite the fact that someone with credit card debt amounting to £2,100, paying 14.9 per cent interest, could be in debt for 27 years if simply paying back the minimum 2 per cent each month that some cards allow.

Daily Mail

There were several days in July 2006 when the temperatures nudged 100 degrees Fahrenheit. Not everybody was pleased and there were the routine complaints about how unsightly Englishmen are in shorts. As if this wasn't offence enough, Jeremy Tozer, of Teignmouth, Devon, wrote: 'The problem is not Englishmen in shorts but Englishmen wearing socks with sandals.'

Brian Haslam, of Watnall, Nottinghamshire, wrote that

the hot weather 'also brings out a greater number of obese Englishwomen in shorts, which is far more disturbing.'

Daily Telegraph

The July 2006 heatwave caused much devastation around the country, but to some the most significant indicator that global warming was getting out of control was reported when some of the nation's most senior judges turned up for work in the Royal Courts of Justice in the Strand – without their wigs.

Guardian

William Langley in the *Sunday Telegraph* had this to say to those who complained about high temperatures during the hot summer of 2006:

'Britain conquered some of the hottest countries in the world and ran them for decades without breaking sweat or removing jackets. No wonder it is said that the collapse of the Empire began with the first man to sit down to dinner in shorts.'

Sunday Telegraph

There are dozens of Acacia Avenues spread all over the country and they have been called 'the nesting box of Middle England'. An AA survey found the recipe for happiness for people who live in these Avenues involves never moving, never divorcing and never changing jobs. They have three bedrooms and a garden in which one in five has a shed and one in ten a garden gnome. For more than half a century Acacia Avenues have evoked comfortable, yet invincible, images of greenery, car washing, community spirit and conformity.

Four out of ten Avenue-dwellers say fish and chips is their favourite meal.

The think-tank Demos announced a Save Suburbia campaign which includes plans to reinvigorate Acacia Avenues by reinventing the Tupperware party and encouraging groups of men to join together in car-washing circles.

The Times/Guardian

It was a day that will go down in history. On 17 October 2006, thousands across Britain documented the details of their day-to-day lives in a mass blog organised by History Matters. Excited historians say it will offer an invaluable snapshot of British life to future generations.

The following day The Times headline covering the event was: 'Happy, sad, bored and even suicidal: a day in the life of Britain's bloggers. Got up, went to work, came home again, watched TV, went to bed.' For most of us, apparently, it was a day of monotony. We commuted to work... and spent the intervening hours thinking of home time.

The Times coverage was illustrated with a cartoon by Pugh showing a middle-aged wife telling her husband: 'Future generations won't want to hear about you sorting out your sock drawer.'

But the organisers were thrilled and one said that each blog was 'really valuable. The entries are all so interesting.'

The Times

Sam Leith in his *Daily Telegraph* Notebook recalls the days of seaside B&Bs: 'Breakfast is 7.30 to 8:00am... Arrive at 8.02 hoping for at least a slice of carbonised toast and the landlady sets her mouth into the cat's bottom position and keeps it there no matter how charming you attempt to be.'

Nevertheless, he continues, 'I have a certain affection for such places. They are an essential part of the fabric of English provincial life.'

Daily Telegraph

Cumbria's tourist office set up a call line so that people could listen in to inviting sounds from the Lakes, such as a reading of Wordsworth's 'Daffodils', the sound of water lapping Windermere's shores – even a Cumberland sausage sizzling in the pan.

Richard Littlejohn in the *Daily Mail* thought London might catch on to the idea and among his suggestions were:

- To hear a young woman vomiting in Soho, press 3.
- To hear aggressive begging, press 4.
- To hear an announcement about your train being cancelled, press 5.
- To hear the sound of police sirens as police

respond to a fracas outside a boozer at chucking-out time, press 6.

- To hear the sound of breaking glass as a drunk has his head shoved through a shop window, press 7.
- If you would like information about emigrating we don't blame you.

Daily Mail

It's positively British – the business of cleaning up before the cleaner arrives. Philip Smith, of Winscombe, Somerset, remembers his mother waking him with: 'Hurry up. Tidy your room. The cleaner is coming.'

Daily Telegraph

Gill Clark, of Wheathampstead, Hertfordshire, writes: 'If you are lucky enough to have a really good cleaner who also tidies up you may never find the items that are tidied away.'

Daily Telegraph

A survey revealed the most often told lies. The result was reassuringly British with fibs showing our reluctance to show our true feelings or to be rude to others. Top of the porkies was:

- 'Nothing's wrong. I'm fine.'

Followed by:

- 'Nice to see you.'

63

- 'Sorry I missed your call.'
- 'I'll give you a ring.'
- 'It's just what I always wanted.'
- 'We'll have to meet up soon.'

The Times, Body & Soul section

Richard Morrison in *The Times* spoke up for the people who have a craving for useful things that have disappeared without trace – or, worse still, been demolished by meddlesome modernisers. Here are some of those items which he deems 'quintessential elements in the British character':

- Pubs on Friday nights for people over 30
- Politicians who did something in their lives before politics
- Libraries that are quiet and have books
- Small kids playing conkers or hopscotch rather than 'chat'n' on their mobiles
- Fish and chips wrapped in newspaper
- Sixpences in Christmas puddings
- Unpretentious pub names
- Weddings where the guests don't watch everything through their camcorders
- The village stocks for louts rather than useless Asbos
- Bus conductors and park keepers.

The Times

A survey of young professionals, commissioned by the Devon-based Ashburton Cookery School, discovered that Britain is 'not a nation of complainers'. Sixty-three per cent said they would rather sit in silence rather than cause a scene by sending back unsatisfactory food.

'We are a nation of acutely self-conscious and modest people,' says the survey.

Guardian

As 2006 faded out the *Daily Mail* dug up a page of figures 'that add up to a unique portrait of a year in all our lives'. They included:

1	The number of medals won by Great Britain at the Turin Winter Olympics
4.4	The average number of sparrows in each British garden
8	The number of years a British woman will spend shopping in her lifetime
20	The percentage of British families who said they ate every evening meal watching TV
22lb	The weight of chocolate eaten by the average Britain in 2006 – a European record
36	The number of boys and girls in Britain called Arsenal
254	The number of umbrellas sold at Wimbledon on the first days of the tennis championships

£55,000 The amount that six of England's World
Cup WAGs spent in one hour in Baden-
Baden's luxury shops

Daily Mail

When cargo spilled from a stricken ship washed up on the beaches of Devon's World Heritage Jurassic shore in January 2007, some reports said that scavengers went into 'a feeding frenzy' – scooping up BMW motorcycles, wine casks, and cases of nappies, dog food and cosmetics.

But a tongue-in-cheek *Times* leader put forward the view that it was 'civic-minded Britons gallantly stepping in to help the vessel's owners in their time of crisis, without waiting to be asked; as briskly as if tidying up the debris on the village green after the annual fête.'

The Times

There was criticism all round about the way two inches of snow had brought chaos to the nation's transport, schools and workplaces. But true British grit emerged in *The Times* letters pages, in a letter from Jacqueline Frampton of Leigh-on-Sea, Essex:

'Sir, Schools paralysed by snowfall? The eldest child in our family eyed the snow in eager anticipation of a snowball extravaganza. And he's only the head teacher.'

The Times

Following a report about 'funny-coloured snow in Siberia', Charles Sandeman-Allen, of Icklesham, East Sussex, reminded Guardian readers of Frank Zappa's warning: 'Watch out where the huskies go and don't eat that yellow snow.'

Guardian

Traditional British ways of life cling on despite the ever-increasing pace of modern life. A *Daily Telegraph* reader wrote to ask if the tea cosy was on its way out. Among the responses which poured in were:

- Sales of cosies rocketed when both fabric and hand-knitted ones were produced at Roz Cundick's craft stall in Hayle, Cornwall.
- Paul Penrose, of Helston, Cornwall, reports that his mother, who owns several tea cosies, suggests tracking them down in retail outlets that stock knitting needles and wool.
- Liz Walmsley, of Addlestone, Surrey, says that an enterprising member of the staff in her husband's office has provided a woolly hat with appropriate holes cut into it.

Daily Telegraph

At a time when every newspaper in the land was banging on about whether we should apologise for having traded in slaves, *Daily Mirror* columnist Brian Reid asked: 'If we start apologising for the sins of our ancestors, where do we stop?' He listed

some fifty things we might want to apologise for –
including 'obscenities we're still giving the world'.
Among them:

- Inventing the internal combustion engine,
  giving rise to Jeremy Clarkson
- John Logie Baird's TV discovery, which
  spawned Simon Cowell
- Alexander Bell for inventing the telephone,
  leading to the phrase: 'It's me. I'm on the
  train.'
- M & S cardigans
- Jeffery Archer books
- Richard Branson's grin
- Bagpipes
- Net curtains
- Marmite
- Gentlemen's clubs
- Paisley ties
- Tweed jackets

Daily Mirror

Chapter 5

MEDIA MADNESS

'A dawn raid by immigration officials on the home of a Turkish Kurd family was called off this morning because they weren't in.'

BBC Radio Scotland

Least surprising story of the year? The most common complaint of sword swallowers is a sore throat.

Observer, quoting the *British Medical Journal*

And another obvious one: 'Police Hunt for Stolen Copper'.
Headline spotted by E. Scullion of Cambridge,
Cambridge Evening News

Guardian diarist Jon Henley said that a headline with a good chance of winning his Headline of the Week Award came from the Agence France Presse, with the intriguing: 'Man Loses Nose in Circumcision Ceremony'.

Guardian

Rupert Murdoch was having his portrait painted by Jonathan Yeo whose premises were being shared with Alison Jackson, famous for her BBC2 lookalike series *Double Take*.

Alison was dealing with doubles for Kylie, Posh and Becks and Elton John when the media tycoon opened the door to be told: 'Sorry mate, we didn't order a Murdoch today.'

Daily Telegraph

When Anna Ford, 62, gave up her BBC News presenter role in 2006 (after 27 years) she said: 'I'll miss the friendship of the viewers. Some have written to me for years. I'm still touched by people who innocently think we can see them. So, my thanks to the woman who wanted me to comment on her new wallpaper.'

Sun

Jane Goody rose to fame on her reputation of being one of the dimmest contestants on Channel 4's *Big Brother* reality contest. She thought Rio de Janeiro was a

person and that Portugal was in Spain. She once said: 'People from Newcastle – they're called Liverpudlians aren't they?'

Sunday Times

Among people who write letters to newspapers there is strong competition to have one chosen for the light-hearted bottom right-hand corner of the Times letters page. They are often witty and hilarious. Make your own judgement on one from Charles Murray, of Workington, Cumbria, who wondered if tawny owls were having a poor breeding season because it was too wet to woo.

The Times

Newspaper articles do not always live up to the Page One blurbs which trumpet features on inside pages.

Stephen Glover, writing in the *Independent*, refers to a *Times* front page puff asking: 'What is the meaning of life? Answer Inside.'

This tease reminded him of a story told by Peter McKay who swears that one Friday he saw a newspaper van carrying the message: 'Is there life after death? Find out in *Monday's Evening Standard*'.

Independent

Famous *Daily Mail* columnist John Edwards writes about an even bigger Fleet Street legend, Fergus Cashin, the late-show business writer of the Daily Sketch.

Fergus knew every joint in the West End that stayed open until dawn – opening hours were anytime he was awake and he greeted each morning as the beginning of a 20-hour challenge to make it more hilarious than the last 20 hours... He interviewed film stars from couches in five-star hotels, the couch often becoming his bed for the night. Anywhere his shoes came off was home.

In Ronnie Scott's jazz club in the sixties Fergus offered to buy a drink for the equally larger-than-life Roland Kirk, a celebrated blind black saxophonist. 'My usual,' said Roland to the barman, who then poured Green Chartreuse into a glass followed by blue curacao, yellow Italian Galliano and more coloured liqueurs.

Fergus paid for the expensive rainbow mixture and said to Roland: 'No wonder you're f*****g blind.'

Daily Mail

The *Guardian* included the following in its Local Newspaper Story of the Week awards:

- **'Twenty Pints of Guinness, Five Alcopops – Then Home on a Cart'. A story in the *Welwyn & Hatfield Times* about a Knebworth farmer, caught drunk in charge of a horse and cart, who** claimed 'It's a lot less safer than being drunk in charge of a car.'

- 'Brief's Brief Briefs Protest'. About a solicitor who faced charges after dropping trousers in a Sunderland court in protest at security measures.

Guardian

In April 2006 Sue Lawley announced that she was leaving *Desert Island Discs* after presenting the BBC's institutional Radio 4 programme for almost nineteen years.

Shortly before taking over the programme in 1987, she herself was the castaway victim – interviewed by Michael Parkinson. The luxury she chose to take with her was an iron and ironing board. When she announced that she was leaving Sue wanted something very different. 'I would like as my luxury,' she said, 'to be bestowed with a very small golf handicap.'

Guardian/Daily Telegraph

In 2006 W. F. Deedes, aged 93, celebrated 75 years in journalism – rising from totally inexperienced cub reporter to become editor of the *Daily Telegraph*.

In 1934 he filed a stinging despatch from Ascot about the failure of gentlemen to wear morning coats.

When asked how he got his first break in journalism he replied: 'Outrageous nepotism.'

Daily Telegraph

Fans of the *Daily Telegraph's* crossword puzzles celebrated the approach of the newspaper's 25,000th puzzle and showed what gluttons they are for punishment. Among the favourites were:

- Clue: HIJKLMNO. Solution: Water
- Clue: Geg. Solution: Scrambled egg
- Clue: You find them in the classrooms. Solution: Schoolmasters
- Clue IST. Solution: Capitalist
- Clue: revo. Solution: overturned

Daily Telegraph

In May 2006 Richard Littlejohn's *Daily Mail* column picked out the following headlines:

- 'Nurseries Ordered to Root Out Racism Among Three-year-olds'
- 'Councils Banning Ice-cream Vans from Operating Near Schools'
- NHS Spending £5,000 a Time Stapling Up the Stomachs of People Too Lazy to Diet'

Daily Mail

Guardian diarist Jon Henley reported on 23 May 2006 that a strong contender for the Local Newsmedia Correction of the Week Award was BBC Scotland, which explained that a wartime bomb found in Liverpool's harbour was 'dropped by the Luftwaffe and not, as our earlier reports said, Lufthansa'.

Guardian

A *Guardian* diary's 'Caption of the Week Award' in October 2006 went to the *Daily Telegraph*. The caption was underneath a picture of George Sugden who won two MCs in North Africa and died in 2006 aged 94. It read:

'Although he had played soccer for Shrewsbury, in France he was accused of being a German spy.'

Guardian

The following definitions have been around for years:
- *The Times* is read by the people who run the country.
- The *Daily Mirror* is read by the people who think they run the country.
- The *Guardian* is read by the people who think they should run the country.
- The *Morning Star* is read by the people who think the country should be run by another country.
- The *Daily Mail* is read by the wives of the people who run the country.
- The *Financial Times* is read by the people who own the country.
- The *Daily Express* is read by the people who think the country should be run as it used to be run.
- The *Daily Telegraph* is read by the people who think it still is.
- The *Sun* is read by the people who don't

care who runs the country as long as she's got big breasts.

Alongside the above an updated version was printed in the *Daily Mail* in October 2006:

- *The Times* is read by the people who think Rupert Murdoch should run the country.
- The *Daily Mirror* is read by the people who think they should run the country.
- The *Guardian* is read by the neo-socialists who actually do run the country.
- The *Morning Star* is read by the people who think we should be run by any country other than America.
- The *Daily Mail* is read by the people who pay for the country.
- The *Financial Times* is read by the people who should pay but keep their wealth out of the country.
- The *Daily Express* is read by the people who think the country should be run by pressure groups and think tanks.
- The *Daily Telegraph* is read by the people who know that it is.
- The *Sun* is read by the people who still don't care who runs the country as long as she's got big breasts.

Submitted by Stephen Green, Great Missenden, Buckinghamshire, *Daily Mail*

In October 2006 it was impossible to get away from headlines warning that global warming was upon us and that the end was nigh. The *Westmoreland Gazette* thought it time to publish a report saying that the month of October had been exceptionally warm and that on the 25th the noon temperature was 67 degrees in the shade.

This particular bit of global warming was first published by the Gazette in 1856.

Westmoreland Gazette

Mastermind chairman John Humphrys says he would no more sit in that terrifying black quiz chair than enter a boxing ring with Big John Prescott.

He once did agree to answer questions in a spoof Mastermind – providing he could choose John Humphrys as his specialist subject. He still didn't get them all right.

Daily Mail

A Japanese TV company is planning a new realty TV show to transform a Japanese celebrity into an English gent. The proposal is to plant him into a posh English family to 'learn about the refined ways of English life and become a master of etiquette'.

Among other things, lessons are planned into how to eat crumpets, put on wellies and greet magpies.

Daily Telegraph

The *Guardian* magazine *G2* celebrated April Fool's day in 2007 with pages of classic examples, such as the following:

In 1976 Patrick Moore announced on TV that a unique astronomical event was going to occur at 9.47am when Pluto would be passing behind Jupiter. This gravitational alignment would reduce the Earth's gravity for a few moments. Anyone who jumped into the air at 9.47 would experience a strange floating sensation.

The BBC was flooded with calls from people claiming to have floated – including one woman who said she and eleven friends had been wafted from their chairs and orbited gently around the room.

Guardian G2

Maureen O'Donnell has been collecting some of the stupid replies contestants give in TV and radio shows:
Question: What was Gandhi's first name?
Answer: Goosey, Goosey? (University Challenge)

Question: Where do you think Cambridge University is?
Answer: Geography isn't my strong point. Beg, Borrow or Steal (BBC2)

Question: In traffic, what 'J' is where two roads meet?
Answer: Jool carriageway? (Weakest Link)

Question: What happened in Dallas on November
22, 1963?
Answer: I don't know, I wasn't watching it then.
GWR FM (Bristol)

Daily Mail

In contrast, W. Newman, of Oldham, Lancashire,
offers what he calls The World's Easiest Quiz, which
includes the questions:
1 When do the Russians celebrate the October
Revolution?

2 What is a camel's hair brush made of?

3 Which animal are the Canary Islands named after?

4 What colour is a purple finch?

5 What colour is the black box in commercial aircraft?

The answers are:
1 November
2 Squirrel fur
3 Dogs
4 Crimson
5 Orange
And Mr Newman asks: 'What do you mean, you
failed?'

Daily Mail

The *Sunday Telegraph* called this 'the shaggiest, most unbelievable Christmas story of all'.

At Santa's Magical Animal Kingdom in Westmeath, Ireland, staff were looking forward to their Christmas feast – but someone forgot to secure the pen of their Bactrian camel Gus.

Gus, 'about the size of a small elephant with large yellow, prominent front teeth', scoffed more than 200 mince pies and all the crisps and sandwiches and was on his sixth can of Guinness by the time staff turned up.

How does a camel open a can of Guinness? 'With no bother at all' said 14-year-old Clodagh Cleary. 'He was biting the tops off with his big strong teeth and sucking up the Guinness. It was brilliant.'

Sunday Telegraph

Chapter 6

ROYAL FLUSH

It is, quite possibly, a treasonable offence even to contemplate what the Queen gets up to in the shower, the *Daily Telegraph*'s Spy column reported. But it felt compelled to share a report from a palace insider that she dons a shower cap given to her by Prince Harry. The cap carries the message: 'Ain't Life a Bitch'.

Daily Telegraph

On one of the rare occasions when the Queen ventured outside her castle on Royal Deeside she popped into a local teashop and was told by a tourist:

'You look awfully like the Queen.'

Her Majesty replied: 'How very reassuring.'

The Times

Earlier it was reported that when Princess Anne called the Prime Minister's wife 'Mrs Blair', the lady from No.10 said:

'Do call me Cherie.'

The ninth in line to the Throne retorted: 'I'd rather not.'

Guardian

The Queen and Prince Philip visited a Picasso exhibition.

She said: 'Why does he want to put two eyes on the same side of the face?'

He said: 'These are the ones that make me feel a bit drunk.'

Sunday Telegraph

This from a photo caption in the *East Anglian Daily Times*: 'Mae Haxton's four-year-old nephew was watching the Queen on TV during the singing of the National Anthem when he said: "Doesn't that lady know the words?" '

East Anglian Daily Times

Dame Helen Mirren picked up two Golden Globe Awards in 2007 for her title roles in the films *The Queen* and *Elizabeth I*.

In 1979 Helen divested all her garments in *Caligula* and is said to be the actress who inspired the quip: 'She's always prepared to keep her clothes on if the part demands it.'

Daily Mail

At the Golden Globes ceremony, 61-yr-old Helen stunned celebs by reminding them: 'I'm still an Essex girl'.

'You can tell', she said, 'when an Essex girl has an orgasm. She drops her fries.'

Sun

Britain's monarchy struggles to adapt to a changing world. It was well into the sixties before radical members of staff suggested that an internal telephone might be a better method of communication than sending a footman with a written message.

Daily Mail

When Queen Elizabeth II ascended the throne, her husband Prince Philip asked advisers: 'What am I expected to do?' People responded by 'sort of looking down and shuffling their feet,' said Philip. 'Any bloody fool can lay a wreath at the thingamy. You don't have to be a genius for that.'

When visiting Canada the Prince was asked what sort of flight he had had.

'Have you ever flown in a plane?' he returned.

'Yes.'

'Well, it was just like that.'

From abridged extracts from *On Royalty*, by Jeremy Paxman, published by Viking, *Daily Mail*

The *Daily Mail* reports how the Queen's husband has a habit of making the news with his gaffes:

- In 1986 he told British students in China: 'If you stay here much longer, you'll be slitty-eyed.'
- In the early nineties he told a Briton living in food-and-drink-loving Hungary: 'You can't have been here long. You haven't got a pot belly.'
- In 1995 he asked a driving instructor in Scotland: 'How do you keep the natives off the booze long enough to get them past the test?'
- Touring a factory in Edinburgh in 1999 he looked at a fuse box and said that it looked 'as though it had been put in by an Indian'.

Daily Mail

As part of the coverage of the Queen's eightieth birthday, the *Independent on Sunday* recalled the occasion when 31-year-old schizophrenic Michael Fagan broke into Buckingham Palace and got into Her Majesty's bedroom.

The Queen was credited with acting calmly and a friend said later: 'She has met so many dotty people that one more made no difference.'

Independent on Sunday

It was the fiftieth anniversary of the Duke of Edinburgh Awards – set up by Prince Philip to encourage children to develop their potential. At the Buckingham Palace reception the Duke was asked if his organisation was still relevant in modern Britain.

'The point is', he replied, 'that young people are the same as they always were – they are just as ignorant.'

Daily Mail

Buckingham Palace's garden parties have been revealed as an almighty bunfight. Guests wolf an average of 14 cakes, sandwiches, scones and ice creams costing £500,000 a year.

There is a theory that some guests might be taking home cakes and scones as souvenirs, but there is bad news for those who think they might snitch a piece of Buck House china. The crockery is plain white with no insignia.

Independent

In May 2006 the Queen visited an exhibition of some of the best headlines of the century. Jeremy Brien, of Bristol, wrote that in the 1970s the Crystal Palace striker Gerry Queen 'figured in one of the great tabloid headlines of all time: "Queen in brawl at Palace."'

The Times

The Ephraim Hardcastle column in the *Daily Mail* reports on a snippet from a book by royal author Sarah Bradford (in private life Viscountess Bangor). It tells of an occasion when Prince Charles's Bentley was out of commission so he asked for the makers to provide another one. The only one available was in Scotland and it was driven throughout the night to Highgrove.

Charles took one look at it and said: 'It's black. I hate black. We'll take the Vauxhall.'

Daily Mail

Pictures of Prince Harry wearing a bowler appeared in practically every newspaper in May 2006 – as part of the 'proper order of dress' for an officer of the Household Cavalry when not in uniform.
James Lock & Co, the Royal hatters in St James's Street, has been in the same family since 1676. The place has hardly changed since Lord Nelson had his final tricorn hat made there a few weeks before the Battle of Trafalgar.

The Prince Regent was another regular – partly because of its convenient back window. He would walk straight through the shop and climb out into Crown Passage – home of his mistress – without being seen. He always bought a hat on the way back, 'so it was good for business', said a salesman.

Sunday Telegraph

'The Queen wears the Crown, but Prince Philip wears the trousers' – this was the strapline over an article celebrating the eighty-fifth birthday of the Duke of Edinburgh in June 2006.

Some Palace staff have been taken aback by the forthright way Philip speaks to Elizabeth. He is reported to have roundly cursed her '14 f***ing dogs' on more than one occasion.

It is said that once, when the Queen repeatedly sucked in her breath at his fast driving, Philip said: 'If you do that once more I shall put you out of the car.'

This balance of power – the Queen in public, the Duke in private – has resulted in some 60 years of steadfast marriage.

Prince Philip's refusal to play by the rules endears him to people who like to think of him as a lovable eccentric – an unpredictable with a tendency to put his foot in it during fusty royal occasions.

Sunday Telegraph

Zillions were spent re-furbishing Ascot racecourse and there was general acclaim about the job that was done. But one VIP was not totally pleased – the Queen. It was reported that the window in the Royal Box was too high for the 5ft 4in monarch and Her Majesty was not able to get a comfortable view, writes the *Sportsman*.

'One palace source said that the Queen was quite angry – and that is royal code for "absolutely furious."'

Daily Telegraph

As part of her eightieth birthday celebrations, the Queen invited 2,000 children to a party at Buckingham Palace:

- Many of the girls guests dressed right royally and 'there were more tiara-adorned princesses than the Palace has witnessed in its 300-year history'.
- There were lots of celebs there to entertain the children, and Karlie Williams, aged 12, from Ebbw Vale, South Wales, said: 'The day was really special. I got to see J. K. Rowling – and the Queen.'
- Lots of characters from children's books were on parade, and Winnie the Pooh was a particularly appropriate guest. He is the same age as the Queen, both having been born in 1925.
- William Duffy, aged 9, said: 'I found the BBC tent and they told me Beckham had scored and England had won. Brilliant.'

The Times/Daily Telegraph/Guardian

Composer Sir Richard Rodney Bennett said on Radio 4 that one of the Queen Mother's favourite musical ditties was 'Auntie Mary had a canary up the leg of her drawers.'

The *Daily Mail*'s Ephraim Hardcastle column, which reported the above, did not take the bawdy ditty any further, saying that some verses were 'rather risqué'. Google fans can find the song under 'Yorkshire History and Folklore'. Here is a shortened version of it:

Auntie Mary, had a canary, up the leg
  of her drawers
She pulled them down for half a crown.
When she farted it departed
Down the leg of her drawers

Buffalo Billy had a ten foot willy
He showed it to the lady next door
She thought it was a snake so she hit it
  with a rake
And now it's only five foot four

Daily Mail

The Queen Mother's former equerry recalls:
- After dancing with Fred Astaire, she said: 'He was quite a good dancer.'
- Sir Ralph Anstruther, a crusty Old Etonian, served in the Queen Mother's household and was a stickler for detail. Etiquette was his forte and he would pick people up on the state of their ties or their shoes. The Queen Mother would say: 'Oh, don't move the napkins or Ralph will get upset' – sometimes in Ralph's presence, just to be a bit naughty.
- The Queen and the Queen Mother often fed biscuits shaped like Hovis loaves to their dogs. If guests were present they would be given biscuits after lunch or dinner. Often the guests would pick up the biscuits to eat. The Queen or

the Queen Mother would say: 'No, no, no, they're for the dogs.' The Royal pair could easily have prevented the confusion, but their naughty streak often got the better of them.

- 'At about 6pm, the Queen Mother would sometimes say: "Are we at the magic hour?" "Yes, ma'am," I would say before popping off to mix her a martini. This consisted of gin with a sensation of vermouth. The vermouth would be poured into the screw top of the bottle and the contents held over the glass to allow vermouth fumes to somehow miraculously be absorbed into the gin. I would then pour the vermouth back into the bottle.'

From *Behind Palace Doors*, by Major Colin Burgess, published by John Blake, *Sunday Times*

Robert Lacey's book *Majesty* reports how, over a period of years, the French press published:
- 63 reports of Queen Elizabeth II's abdication
- 77 reports of her divorce from Prince Philip
- 115 reports royal quarrels with Lord Snowdon
- 17 reports of rudeness to foreign royalty
- 92 reports of Elizabeth being pregnant.
- As far as is known, only two stories proved to be correct, both about her being pregnant.

Reader's Digest

The *Daily Express* published extracts from a book on how history is littered with rulers and nobles who earned derogatory nicknames.

The lead item was Edward VII (1901–1910), known as Edward the Caresser and described as a fat and unapologetic hedonist.

At Cambridge Edward developed an appetite for food, cigars, gambling – and female company. His long list of mistresses included Lillie Langtry and Sarah Bernhardt. Edward enjoyed eating five large meals a day, often consisting of ten or more courses. By the time he was middle-aged he had a waist of forty-eight inches and earned another nickname: Edward the Wide.

When a guest turned up at Sandringham without the correct evening dress he was made to dine in his bedroom.

From *Fat, Bald and Worthless*
by Robert Easton, published by Penguin, *Daily Express/National Archives*

Following the news that the formidable Princess Royal was to visit Afghanistan, *Times* cartoonist Peter Brookes showed warriors armed with machine guns fleeing as she approached their mountain hide-out shouting: 'NAFF ORFF!'

The Times

In his published diaries the blind former Home Secretary David Blunkett has this February 2001 item referring to the time when he sat next to the Queen at an official lunch:

'She asked me if I would like my meat cutting up... and said: "I often do it for the corgis."'

Extract from *The Blunkett Tapes*, published by
Bloomsbury/*Guardian*

Colonel of The Blues and Royals, Princess Anne spoke at the launch of *Horse Guards, a History of the Household Cavalry* by Barney White-Spunner. Forthright as ever, she opened up with: 'At these events it is normal to remind guests to switch off their mobiles. Here, though, it would be more appropriate to ask guests to make sure their hearing aids are switched on.'

Tim Walker, *Sunday Telegraph*.

Go on, be honest. How many of you know more than the first verse of our National Anthem? They know it in Latvia and it brought some discomfort to Prince Philip when he and the Queen were there in October 2006.

As a local choir reached the end of the first verse the Duke of Edinburgh 'adopted the half-shut penknife position as he lowered himself back towards his chair. Suddenly, in mid-squat, the choir boomed out the second verse.'

The Duke, aged 85, went into reverse and remained

standing. After the third verse finished Philip asked in a stage whisper: 'Is that all?'

Mercifully it was, and the Queen's husband bit his lip and tried not to laugh. Foreign Secretary Margaret Beckett struggled to stifle a giggle.

The *Daily Express* loyally printed 'Your Cut-out and Keep Guide to the National Anthem, Sir.' All FIVE verses.

Daily Express

John Cornwell, a former deputy leader of the South Yorkshire County Council, has written a book, *Tomb of the Unknown Alderman*. He tells of a visit to Sheffield by the Queen and Prince Philip in the 1970s. The city's then Lord Mayor, Martha Strafford, led the royal couple to a waiting line of limousines. Prince Philip headed for the Mayoral Rolls but Martha stopped him, saying:

'That one's mine, love. Yours is the funeral car behind,' pointing to a Co-op limousine.

Sun's Whiplash column/*Yorkshire Post*

'Did I get the ears right, Sir,' was the headline the *Daily Mail* used alongside a sketch of the Prince of Wales by eight-years-old Hugo Marsh, of Davenies School in Beaconsfield, Buckinghamshire. It showed the prince with almost Dumbo-sized ears.

The Mail's assessment of Hugo's artistic efforts was: 'The nose was wonky and the hair a little on the sparse side, but the ears were perfect.'

Prince Charles giggled when he saw the red crayon sketch, and Hugo said later: 'I think it looks like him.'

Daily Mail

Clarence House denied a story saying that Prince Charles' staff would boil seven eggs – from runny soft to rock hard – to make sure that one of them would be to his liking.

Nevertheless the story got international coverage after appearing in Jeremy Paxman's book *On Royalty*.

The *Guardian* had a page one story with a picture of seven boiled eggs. One commentator on the net said it had to be true because 'You Couldn't Make It Up'.

Guardian

Loyal subjects gave flowers to the Queen when she opened their new Jubilee Library in Brighton in March 2007. But two-year-old Lucas Whisker reversed the process when he walked boldly up to Her Majesty and asked for one of her blooms. She put a pink tulip into his hand.

Daily Telegraph

At Sandringham a band had just finished playing the National Anthem.

'I must thank the bandmaster,' said King George VI.

'I have done so,' said an equerry.

'Not quite the same thing,' said His Majesty.

Daily Mail

A St James's Palace wedding reception was attended by Queen Mary, the widow of George V. When Sir Compton Mackenzie, author of Whisky Galore, arrived, he bowed to the wedding cake, mistaking it for the old Queen.

Daily Telegraph

Elvis Presley impersonator Geraint Benney of Aberdare says he has been getting death threats because he is bald. Fans complain that he shows disrespect but Geraint says being bald makes him stand out.

Sunday Times

Chapter 7

RUDE BRITANNIA

'Woman in the throes of passion swallows her lover's dentures.'

Independent on Sunday

Three out of ten British men would be prepared to abstain from sex for life in return for £1 million. Three per cent would do the same if their football team won the treble.

Survey for Durex and *Company* magazine

Artist David Hockney knew he was gay from an early age. 'I was in a cinema aged 13,' he remembers. 'A man took my hand and put it on his cock. I never told my parents, but I've loved the cinema ever since.'

Times Magazine

A mayor accused of sexual discrimination against a female town clerk told an employment tribunal: 'I became infatuated with her as we stood looking at a wall map of Chard.'

Daily Telegraph

Following correspondence about sexual harassment on London Underground a *Guardian* reader writes: 'Upon seeing a man expose himself I said what a friend had advised: 'Hey! That looks like a penis, only smaller!' It worked.

Guardian

The top of a list of chat-up lines compiled by *FHM* magazine was:

'I suffer from amnesia. Do I come here often?'

Number 5 in the list was:

'Is your surname Jacobs? Because, girl, you're a cracker.'

Number 27 was:

'God you're ugly – but I bet you feel good in the dark.'

Sunday Times

There used to be an awful schoolboy joke about a book called *Forty Years in the Saddle* by Major Bumsore. But, wrote the *Financial Times* diarist, 'now I see that there really is an equestrian book called Sixteen Hands Between Your Legs'.

Financial Times

Prostitutes in Oxford have started riding bicycles to fool police into thinking that they are ordinary members of the public.

The Times

Author Alain de Botton says in his book *The Consolations of Philosophy* that sex forces us to abandon sensible plans in order to lie in bed sweating and letting out intense sounds reminiscent of hyenas calling out to one another across the barren wastes. This inspired the *Daily Mail* to fill a page with some of the wittiest quotes on sex:

- Actor Billy Crystal: 'Women need a reason to have sex. Men just need a place.'
- Edgar Wallace: 'An intellectual is someone who has found something more interesting than sex.'
- American comedian Jeff Foxworthy: 'Getting married for sex is like buying a 747 for the free peanuts.'

Daily Mail

The summer of 1911 produced temperatures approaching 100 degrees Fahrenheit and Britain sweltered through the hottest summer of the century so far. Warning of the dangers of such unusual weather, *The Times* introduced a column under the heading 'Deaths From Heat'. Meanwhile necklines plunged, whalebone corsets gave way to the bra and petticoats and bloomers that had protected women's modesty for centuries were removed. Bathing costumes began to shrink – with brave pioneers appearing in swimsuits ending at the elbow rather than the wrist.

The normally reserved British took this sartorial liberation one step further. Under a headline 'The Summer Britain Discovered Sex', the *Daily Mail* (19 June 2006) reviewed a book by Juliet Nicholson entitled *The Perfect Summer: Dancing Into Shadow In 1911*. This described how the relentless heat was accompanied by a rise in libido and unprecedented sexual liberation, especially among the aristocracy. Extra-marital affairs were commonplace and it is reported that Lord Charles Beresford leapt on to a bed where he thought his mistress lay, only to find a startled Bishop of Chester.

The Times/Daily Mail

In July 2006 the Government announced that it was cutting the VAT rate on condoms from 17.5 per cent to 5 per cent. Caroline Flint, the Public Health Minister, said: 'Safe sex has never been cheaper.'

Independent

Giles Oakley, of London, has a friend who is a nurse with an effective response to flashers. When a man exposed himself outside the hospital she said: 'Oh, put that away. I've been handling bigger ones than that all day.'

Guardian

The caring Durex condom company is to market condoms for kids as young as 13 – 49mm wide compared to 55mm for grown-ups.

Sun

Wigan Council advertised for a 'Condom Coordinator' – to give cards to children as young as 13 to take to their school nurse who will issue them with condoms.

Daily Express/Sunday Telegraph

Bournemouth police arrested a kerb-crawling driver after he picked up a prostitute and was about to 'get down to sexual activity'.

The police decided that a reprimand was more suitable than a court appearance because of the man's age.

He was 95.

Guardian/Daily Mail

In November 2006 it was reported that more than 100 people were receiving their State pension early after changing sex to become women.

The Times

A Wakefield woman who deliberately annoyed her neighbours with 'loud sexual groans' got an Asbo ordering her to stop it.

Daily Telegraph

Men ringing a sex chat line at £1.50 a minute thought they were talking to blonde stunner Ashley wearing a lacy bra and thong. In reality they were getting through to a housewife more likely to answer the phone in a tracksuit and comfy slippers.

She was being paid 15p a minute (18p after 2am) and it was her job to keep the fantasists talking for as long as possible. Some callers made unspeakable suggestions but she could still 'prattle on for hours while doing the ironing, washing up or watching *EastEnders* with the sound down'.

Sun

The *Sun* got all excited and filled a whole page with a well-illustrated story revealing that Page Three Girls have been exposing themselves since 1604 (or 'Sixteen Hundred and Phwoarh', as the Sun put it). It told how Charles I's wife had a nipple-revealing dress and reproduced a 1600s woodcutting of a lady flashing her charms. There was also a sexier modern version of Page Three Girl Nicola doing much the same, but better.

There was no room for anything else on Page Three that day.

Sun

Chapter 8

POLITICS: ORDER, ORDER!

Former spy chief Eliza Manningham-Buller admitted that when MI5 first published its telephone number in 1998, most of its callers were people wanting flatpack furniture.
Sun

In February 2007 details were published on how much MPs claimed on their expenses (one lady MP claimed £16,612 for car travel – enough to get her twice around the globe).

Jasper Gerard in the *Observer* commented that journalists complaining about expense fiddling were like skunks complaining about air quality. He then told this story about a journo being asked by his editor if he had enjoyed his lunch with Ian Paisley.

'Most enjoyable, thanks,' replied the hack.

'Hungry, was he? I ask because I had lunch with him on the same day.'

'The greedy b*****d!' came the quick response.

Observer

Harold Macmillan said of the House of Lords:

'If, like me, you are over 90, frail, on two sticks, half-dead and half blind, you stick out like a sore thumb in most places – but not in the House of Lords. Besides, they seem to have a bar and a loo within 30 yards in any direction.'

Daily Telegraph

When the late Enoch Powell was asked by his barber how he liked his haircut, he replied: 'In silence'.

Submitted by Michael Moss, of Ickenham, Middlesex, *Daily Mail*

When the late Alan Clark was asked if he had wasted his life on wine, women and song, he replied: 'Song?'

Simon Hoggart, *Guardian*

Jon Henley reported in his *Guardian Diary* a comment said to have been overheard in the office of Boris Johnson.

The Tory MP for Henley-on-Thames was asked 'by a conscientious constituent to support a major bill now before Parliament aimed at imposing a minimum of corporate social responsibility on British companies'.

'I am,' remarked Bozza sagely, 'savagely opposed to this sort of bollocks.'

Guardian

When Tory party leader David Cameron boosted his green credentials by going on a dog-sled trip in Norway, journalists described his journey as 'emission-free'.

Jo Livingston, of Belvedere, Kent, wrote to say: 'They've obviously never travelled behind a string of huskies.'

The Times

Rory Bremner reports that Michael Howard's election expenses included £3,600 for make-up. This meant, said the impressionist, that the former leader of the Tory party spent more on looking like Michael Howard than he, the mimic, did.

New Statesman

Winston Churchill said: 'History will be kind to me for I intend to write it.'

Submitted by P. Davies, Whitstable, Kent, *Guardian*

This got Jon Henley's Quote of the Week Award in his *Guardian Diary*.

A farmer speaking on BBC Radio 4's was asked to comment on the Department for the Environment, Food and Rural Affairs' lamentable performance on agricultural payments.

'I don't know why they call it the Westminster Village,' he said. 'Where I come from villages have only one idiot.'

Guardian

The Dull Men's Club is devoted to not getting out much and doing nothing very interesting.

John Major was awarded honorary membership, but this was rescinded when news of his affair with Edwina Currie broke.

Independent on Sunday

When Charles de Gaulle visited the Sussex house of Harold Macmillan, a container of his blood was carried by his entourage in case of an assassination attempt.

The French officials wanted to store the blood in the kitchen fridge, but Harold's cook refused, saying 'It's full of haddock.'

Daily Mail

At the Labour Party's conference in Manchester in September 2006 Cherie Blair was reported to have made a gaffe about Gordon Brown's integrity.

Her husband, making his valedictory speech, joked: 'At least I don't have to worry about her running off with the bloke next door.'

The *Guardian* said that Blair was indebted to Les Dawson for the joke and that the comedian's original quip was: 'My wife ran away with the bloke next door. I'm really going to miss him.'

Guardian

Deputy Prime Minister John Prescott created a mini-sensation when he called President Bush's policies 'Crap'. But, the *Independent* reminded its readers, it was hardly up there with some of the great insults:

- Martin Luther said Henry VIII was 'a pig, an ass, a dunghill, the spawn of an adder, a basilisk, a lying buffoon, a mad fool with a frothy mouth, a frantic madman'.
- General Charles Lee thought that George Washington was a 'dark designing, sordid, ambitious, vain, proud, arrogant, a vindictive knave'.
- Jonathan Aitken said on Margaret Thatcher's grasp of policy: 'I wouldn't say she is open-minded on the Middle East, so much as empty-headed. She probably thinks Sinai is the plural of sinus.'

Independent

Photographs of Prime Minister Tony Blair on his 2006 holiday in the Caribbean revealed what *The Times* called his man-boobs (or moobs).

Michele Kirsch in Times 2 wrote that 'while it is obviously too late for Mrs Blair to heed my mother's advice ('Never marry a man whose tits are bigger than yours') – there was still time for him to exercise and put the tone back into Tony. Maybe not jogging. Men with moobs don't like jogging for obvious reasons.'

(In 2005 the St George's and Princess Grace hospitals in London performed 150 breast reduction surgeries – on men.)

The Times

Amid a blizzard of reports revealing chaos at the Home Office, the *Guardian Diary* of 25 May 2006 carried a helpful note for new Home Secretary John Reid in case he was 'wondering where his staff are… They're currently benefiting from the Home Office's valuable Adult Education Week, having taken time off for hourly classes that include Learning to Waltz, Introducing Home Office Women, Painting for Beginners, Learning Japanese, and Wicca: A Guide to Witchcraft… The words "couldn't", "make", "you", "up" and "it" may not be entirely out of place.'

Guardian

Government chauffeurs have a monthly massage to soothe away the cares and strains of the job.

Sunday Times

One of the problems faced by the new Home Secretary in 2006 was the high number of escaped prisoners – particularly from open jails.

A former inmate told of his time in one of them when a new arrival 'took one look at the dreadful accommodation on offer, ordered a taxi and was gone in 20 minutes'.

So many prisoners went 'over the fence' that it was dubbed 'The Grand National.'

Sunday Times

At the Hay-on-Wye literary festival in 2006 Lord Patten, former Tory minister and Hong Kong governor, told a story about a recent Home Secretary who visited Wormwood Scrubs prison and opened his address with: 'It's so good to see so many of you here today.'

Sun

Deputy Prime Minister John Prescott took a lot of stick after being photographed playing the 'posh' game of croquet.

He said afterwards: 'I don't know the rules. Isn't it to put the ball through the hoop and beat the other bugger?'

Guardian

In the same edition the *Guardian* had a diary item on croquet quoting the view that 'it has long been a commonplace amongst the mallet men that the Victorian ploy of hitting your nubile partner's ball into the shrubbery as a preliminary to sexual dalliance remains one of the principal attractions of the game'.

Guardian

The *Daily Telegraph* carried an article referring to Mr Prescott's celebrated joke of 1996: 'I no longer keep coal in the bath. I keep it in the bidet.'

The article praised the sophistication of the humour, but it was followed by a letter from Sandra McGregor, of Emsworth, Hampshire, saying: 'The line was from that week's News Huddlines on Radio 2. I know – because I scripted the gag.'

Daily Telegraph

Eric Forth, Tory MP for Bromley & Chislehurst, died aged 61 in May 2006. His obituaries described him as tall, dark, lean, flamboyant and a combative Right-wing libertarian and a most effective tormentor of Labour ministers.

He was in favour of capital punishment and implacably opposed to equal opportunities.

He was quoted as saying at a private dinner: 'There are millions of people in this country who are white, Anglo-Saxon and bigoted and they need to be represented.'

The Times / Telegraph

A reader wrote to the *Independent* in July 2006 about 'the backlog of asylum and immigration cases outgrowing the ability of the State to cope... being part of a 20-year culture of governments which have forgotten how to govern.'

Quite so. They knew how to cope much better in the 1970s – as demonstrated by a *Times* letter published on the same day.

Sir Robert Andrew writes that when he worked in the Home Office some 30 years ago he asked what was being done about a large backlog of unanswered letters in the Immigration and Nationality Department at Croydon. He was told that a standard letter was being introduced aimed at speeding up the system. The letter said:

> Sir
> *I am directed by the Secretary of State to acknowledge receipt of your letter of the 15th and to inform you that it is not one of those which has been selected for reply.*

Independent/The Times

Winston Churchill used to scribble 'KBO' (Keep Buggering On) in the margins of State papers.

The Times

Years after leaving Downing Street Ted Heath met the philosopher Sir Anthony Kenny, former head of Heath's old college, Balliol.

When Heath addressed Kenny as 'Master' Kenny joked:' If you keep calling me Master, I shall have to call you Prime Minister.'

'Oh', said Heath, 'I should like that very much.'

Independent

Sir George Young, Tory MP for North West Hampshire, says:

'If you want to irritate an MP – a popular national pastime – you refer to his or her three-month summer holiday. However, just because the House is not sitting, it does not mean we are sipping pints at the local, watching the cricket or doing killer sudoku. The House of Commons sits longer than almost any other legislature – and, to judge from constituents critical of our output, the fewer days we sit the less damage we do.'

From *The Whip* column in the *Sun*, which adds the comment: Hear, hear!

Those who fear public speaking should take comfort from Winston Churchill, who considered only two things more difficult than speaking well in public:

- Climbing a wall that is leaning towards you
- Kissing a woman leaning away from you

Submitted by Henry Clark, Melton Mowbray, Leicestershire, *Financial Times*

When the Home Office make a cock up they do it BIG. One of their financial shambles resulted in an accounting system producing figures showing transactions of more than £26 TRILLION – a figure which is one and a half times higher than the GDP of the planet.

The National Audit Office was inspired to report that 'this suggests something has gone seriously awry'.

Richard Bacon, a Tory member of the Commons Public Accounts Committee said: 'You might reasonably expect to see this in a Gilbert and Sullivan opera, but not in real life... In any parish council or cricket club the person responsible would have been out on his ear. What actually happened was that Sir John Gieve [former HO permanent secretary] was promoted to become Deputy Governor of the Bank of England.'

The Times

The Freedom of Information Act does not quite give total freedom to all information.

A request for access to any letters written by Prince Charles to John Prescott was answered with this from the Office of the Deputy Prime Minister:

'The public interest in preserving [the Prince of Wales's] constitutional position outweighs the general public interest consideration in favour of acknowledging the existence or non-existence of correspondence between this Office and HRH the Prince of Wales. This should not, however, be taken as an indication that the information requested is or is not held by this Office.'

Guardian

Nine-year-old Kieran Williams released a balloon at his school fête in Catcott, Somerset, and it landed 150 miles away – in the garden of the Prime Minister's country retreat at Chequers.

Keiran got his balloon back along with a signed photograph of Tony Blair and his wife and a note written by Cherie: 'Look who found your balloon!'

Daily Mirror

Foreign Secretary Margaret Beckett and her husband Leo went on holiday in France in August 2006 – in their £11,820 caravan. Three Special Branch 'minders' accompanied them in a £45,000 state-of-the-art motorhome.

Daily Mail

When will Blair stand down? Will he be succeeded by Gordon Brown? These were the hot political questions as other Labour wannabes joined the queue of possible contenders in September 2006. But nobody was expected to emulate the Duke of Wellington – the only British Prime Minister to fight a duel while in office.

Daily Express

In a list of 'Ten Things You Never Knew About Prime Ministers', the *Daily Express* included:

- Alec Douglas-Home – the only one to have played first-class cricket
- Spencer Perceval – the only one to be assassinated (in 1812)
- John Bute whose previous role – before he became PM in 1762 – was Groom of the Stole to the future King George III, a job entailing carrying the royal chamber pot on long journeys

Daily Express

When Andrew Gimson asked Boris Johnson if he could write his biography, the Conservative MP for Henley-on-Thames and former editor of the Spectator said: 'Such is my colossal vanity that I have no intention of trying to forbid you.'

Boris also said: 'If it's a piss-take that's OK... but anything that purported to tell the truth really would be intolerable.'

Sunday Times

When the Old Vic's artistic director Kevin Spacey appeared on Michael Parkinson's chat show along with Tony Blair, the veteran interviewer said: 'At your school... you were called the best actor of your generation.'

He was referring, needless to say, to the Prime Minister.

Sunday Telegraph

Winston Churchill was first elected a Conservative in 1900. He defected to the Liberals in 1904 and rejoined the Tories in 1925.

He said: 'It takes a certain ingenuity to re-rat.'

Guardian

This joke does not really qualify to be in a book of true stories, but it does give a real-life view of what many fondly think about Cherie Blair.

Cherie tells Tony that he got his first date with her because she tossed a coin to decide whether to go out with him or another bloke who was now managing a petrol station.

'You mean,' says Tony, 'that if the coin had spun the other way you would now be married to a petrol station manager?'

'No,' she replies, 'he would have become Prime Minister.'

Submitted by Ron Mitchell, Cheshunt, Hertfordshire, *Daily Mail*

Richard Littlejohn didn't think much of Government plans for dealing with absent fathers who fail to pay child maintenance. They included naming and shaming them on the internet and compelling errant fathers to put their names on children's birth certificates.

It all reminded him of Trigger in *Only Fools and Horses* getting sight of his birth certificate.

Under 'Father's Name' it said: 'Some soldiers'.

Daily Mail

On 4 December 2006 Norman Baker, the Rt. Hon. Member for Lewes, had submitted a written question asking the Government to make a statement on the future of the Tate. The Government, slightly mystified, assured him that the Tate was safe.

Four days later Mr Baker asked for a statement on the future of the Tote.

Guardian

Gordon Brown tells the following story against himself. When he was a new MP he was invited to speak to a Scottish pensioners' group. He asked the chairman for how long he should speak and heard the instruction: '45 minutes'.

Dutifully, Brown droned on and on about pensions and when he sat down the chairman addressed the audience, saying: 'And now, friends, there's not enough time for any other speakers'.

Brown said: 'Look, I thought you said 45 minutes?
The chairman said: 'Four to five minutes.'

Independent on Sunday

Shadow Home Secretary David Davis's favourite joke:

I saw an MP who had just been made a minister rushing through the Members' Lobby just after the 1987 election.

I said to him: 'Slow down. Rome wasn't built in a day.'

He said: 'Margaret Thatcher wasn't on that job.'

Daily Telegraph's Spy column

A *Guardian* writer wondered if the sculpture of Baroness Thatcher in the House of Commons might not have been bigger.

Antony Dufort, the sculptor, responded that it had to be on the same scale as the three prime ministers already in the members' lobby.

He pointed out that, at 7ft 4⅜in, Margaret is, in fact, taller than Churchill (7ft 3¼in), Attlee (7ft 3½in), and Lloyd George (7ft).

The Baroness, writes Mr Dufort, has the advantage of high heels over all three – and hair over the first two.

Guardian

The Times printed a full page of 59 things that would have stayed secret but for the Freedom of Information Act. They included:

- Tony Blair spent nearly £2,000 of taxpayers' money on cosmetics over six years.
- Two hundred serving police officers have criminal records for offences that include assault, breach of the peace, theft and vandalism.
- Tax inspectors are routinely offered bonuses to encourage them to collect as much money as possible.

The Times

The *Sunday Times* Atticus column asks: 'What does it say about our attitude to politics when an online petition to Downing Street calling for intervention in Zimbabwe gets 2,474 signatures – but a call for Blair to stand on his head while juggling ice cream collects 4,492?

Sunday Times

Soon after the power-sharing agreement in Northern Ireland in March 2007 Sinn Fein's online store stopped selling mugs carrying the message: 'Still An Unrepentant Fenian Bastard'.

Sun

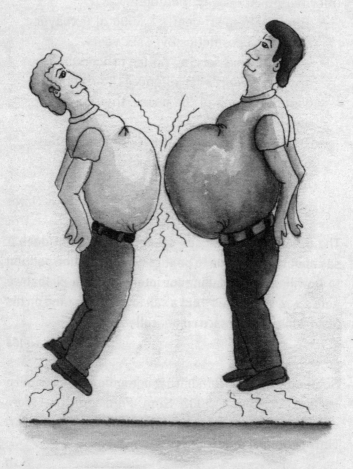

A national poll reveals that one third of British men have a beer gut. What's more, 7 per cent of those polled expressed pride at having one.

Independent on Sunday

Chapter 9

ANIMAL MAGIC

A Canadian woman arrived home to find a bear eating porridge in her kitchen.

Independent on Sunday

Colin Barker, of Southend, Essex, tells of the day when his younger son Julian was about six. The family bull terrier, called Blossom, left its droppings on the lawn and Colin's visiting father-in-law went out to clean up.

He said to Julian: 'Who usually does this, your father?'

'No,' the boy replied, 'The dog does it.'

Daily Mail

English lambs were clipped to look like poodles and sold at high prices to rich Japanese. The scam was rumbled when a Japanese movie star complained that her poodle refused to bark or eat dog food.

Sun

Welsh tortoise recaptured 1.8 miles from home after eight months on the run.

Independent on Sunday

Ratty the terrier used to trot down to the bus stop by himself, jump aboard a No.10 bus into York and get off at the Black Bull pub in York where he was greeted with bangers and kitchen scraps. He was foiled when the pub changed hands and banned dogs.

But the canny canine continued to take the No.10 bus, jump off at the same stop and head across the road to the Rose and Crown, where he is greeted with sausages and scraps.

'He's welcome here anytime,' says landlord Paul Clary.

Sun/Guardian

The threat of eviction hung over a York family after neighbours complained that Sparky, their parrot, sits in the window squawking at passers-by: 'Show us your knickers.'

Independent on Sunday

Guardian diarist Jon Henley found it heartening that on a day 'when half of Baghdad was blown to bits and our proud nation grappled with profound issues of racism, bigotry and Chelsea's lack of a central defence', Andrew Pelling, Tory MP for Croydon Central, tabled an Early Day Motion expressing sympathy for Rick Stein and his family on the passing away of Chalky, the Jack Russell terrier which co-starred in the chef's TV appearances.

Guardian

Tina, a 54-year-old, three-legged tortoise at Longleat Safari Park in Wiltshire, has had a wheel and a suspension system fitted. She is one of the park's oldest tortoises — but is now among the fastest there.

The Times

A snail called Archie won the 1995 World Snail Racing Championship in Congham, Norfolk, by covering 13 inches in two minutes, 20 seconds — at a pace of 0.0005mph.

Reader's Digest

Just before Christmas 2006 Colin Campbell of South Shields spotted a live lobster moving among the ice on a fishmonger's counter. He paid £18 for the delicious crustacean and took it to the local pier. 'I undid his nipper restraints and popped him back into the sea to join his mates,' he said. 'He was a lucky lobster and the good feeling I had was worth the £18 I paid for him.'

Daily Mail

Two piglets called Rupert and Penny are being taught to play the piano by Katie Mason, 25, of Devon.
   Katie is studying animal behaviour and says: 'Rupert is quicker at learning and his sister Penny copies him.'

The Times

Tybalt, a kitten of little brain, escaped from its first experience of snow by taking shelter under the roof of Mr A. V. G. Hagedorn's bird table in Chelmsford, Essex.

Daily Mail

Exmoor Zoo in Devon got fed up with thieves stealing their tiny marmoset monkeys. So they moved in some vicious baboons and said: 'If these people want to break in now they would be lucky to get out in once piece.'

Times

When London Zoo erected a sign saying: 'Annual Stock Take. Please Queue Here', *The Times* published a picture of the sign with a line of Jackass penguins obediently forming a queue.

The Times

During the football fever of the 2006 World Cup, the 120-strong troop of baboons at Knowsley Safari Park switched from stealing windscreen wipers and turned their attention to England flags. 'They've built up quite a selection,' said an official.

Liverpool Echo

A peacock called Mr. P fell in love with a petrol pump in the Forest of Dean, Gloucestershire.
Shirley Horsman, the bird's owner, said: 'The clicking of the pump makes the same noise as a peahen crying 'Come on, I'm ready'. So every time he hears someone filling up he thinks he is on to a good thing.'

For the past three years Mr P has taken to walking from his woodland home to the nearby Brierley service station to parade his plumage and 'get very amorous'.

Daily Telegraph

Concert-goers at the summer music festival at Hampton Court complained that items from their picnics had been pilfered. A CCTV recording, however, revealed that the villain was a resident duck – now nicknamed Robin.

A bemused guest said: 'I suppose it makes sense. All my smoked salmon sandwiches were gone, but the duck pâté was left.'

Daily Telegraph

A black and white cat called Simon is the most highly decorated cat in military history. He was remembered in July 2006 at an exhibition at the Imperial War Museum, London, celebrating animal courage in times of war.

Simon was the rat-catcher on *HMS Amethyst* when the warship was attacked on the Yangtze river by Chinese communists in 1949. He is the only cat to win the Dickin Medal (the 'Animals' VC'). He was hit by shrapnel but continued his rat-catching duties and helped boost morale on board. A 'Cat Officer' was appointed to cope with Simon's fan mail which included hero-worshipping poems – and also bits of fish.

Other animals featured in the exhibition were:

- Winkie, a pigeon who saved the lives of an aircrew ditched at sea by carrying home details of their position
- Roselle, a Labrador, who guided her blind owner from the seventy-eighth floor of the World Trade Center destroyed by terrorists in 2001

The Times

Is another grand old British tradition dying? Firemen being called out to rescue cats from trees has always been part of the rich fabric of life for a pet-loving nation. But the firefighters of Carlisle refused to rescue three-year-old Lilly who was stranded 40ft up a sycamore tree.

'Too dangerous,' they said. 'The risks far outweigh the benefits.'

Owner Liz Bailey got an RSPCA tree surgeon to get Lilley down with ropes, a harness and a basket.

Sun

A burglar was bitten by a macaw named Mickey when he tried to steal the bird from a pet shop in Frome, Somerset. DNA from the blood drawn by Mickey identified the thief and magistrates remanded him in custody.

Owner Angus Hart said that 50-year-old Mickey was 'a miserable git with a vicious temper'.

Sun

Too many British dogs prefer an easy life as cosseted pets and police are having to import their dogs from countries where canines are made to work. Sgt Jim Gall, head of dog training for the South Wales police says: 'Some British dogs just want to put their feet up in front of the telly.'

Sunday Telegraph

Rodney Trotter was a cute piglet when he became a pet of the Barwick family. They all fell in love with him, including Barney their poodle.

But Rodney is not a miniature breed as was thought – he is a Large Middle White boar and has grown into a 25-stone monster too big for the

Barwick's small back garden in Newport, Gwent. In 2006 they began looking for a new home for Rodney – but it must be somewhere where they can visit him.

Daily Express

A Doberman Pinscher called Barney was hired to guard an exhibition of valuable teddy bears at Wookey Hole Caves in Somerset. Barney's CV includes six years of blameless service but an inexplicable something triggered him into rampaging among the cuddly toys. 'Up to 100 bears were involved in the massacre,' said an official. 'It was a dreadful scene.'

Among the savaged bears was one which used to belong to Elvis Presley – loaned to the exhibition by a Presley fan who paid £40,000 for it.

The Times, under the headline 'He ain't nothing but a guard dog'/*Daily Mail* and *Guardian*, under the headline 'All shook up'

Swimmer Paul Westlake, 30, thought he had seen the last of his wallet when it fell into the sea in Plymouth Sound. A few days later a local diver brought a lobster to the surface and found Paul's wallet in the firm grip of one of its claws.

A grateful Paul said: 'I have never eaten a lobster and I never will now.'

Western Morning News

128

What's the best way to get rid of mice? *Daily Telegraph* readers could not agree.

- S. Gibbons of London SW5 said London mice were too sophisticated to fall for traps and said there was only one way: 'It's called a cat.'
- Wendy Bendig, of London SW1, said: 'What a pity to resort to a cat. Knightsbridge mice willingly self-destruct on chocolate.'
- Robert and Karen Mayhew, of Dersingham, Norfolk, said chocolate raisins never fail.
- Marcus White, of Sleaford, Lincolnshire, boasted: 'My mousetrap caught 26 on the same piece of mature Cheddar.'
- Hamish Halls, of Yelverton, Devon, advised: 'Forget the cheese. Mice go for Bath Olivers.'
- David Pearce, of Chesterfield, Derbyshire, found that the head of a Swan Vesta match was the most successful: 'Mice cannot resist the sulphur.'
- David Vaughan, of Welford, Northamptonshire, used bacon rind tied to the trap with fuse wire: 'One hundred per cent success rate.'
- Jean Parker, of Towcester, Northamptonshire, goes for peanut butter.

Daily Telegraph

Mary Richards, columnist in the *Cornish Times*, tells of the animal care home which found a small crocodile left on its doorstep along with a note saying: 'Sorry. He bit the missus.'

Cornish Times

Police dog handler Derek Darling came across a lone piglet while patrolling in the New Forest with his Alsatian, Ash. The pig ran off as they approached – and then returned along with nine angry pigs and piglets.

'They circled around us and, in a sort of military-style manoeuvre, made an arrowhead formation and charged. The only thing we could do was make a run for it,' said PC Darling. The chase lasted about half a mile before Derek and Ash reached the safety of their police car.

'We were hopelessly outnumbered,' said Derek.

The Times

A Yorkshire couple who split up eased the pain of their parting by thrashing out a custody agreement giving them both access to their three pet rats.

Daily Telegraph

Chris Evans, of Windermere, Cumbria, wrote to the Queen to tell her that his cat Flook was nearing its sixteenth birthday – the equivalent of a human's 100 years. To his astonishment he received a letter from Buckingham Palace telling him how interested the

Queen was to learn that Flook had had reached such a remarkable age and hoping that he had enjoyed celebrating its birthday.

'I never expected a reply,' said Chris.

Daily Mail

Dog lover Judith Summers went to the Kennel Club's annual Discover Dogs show in November 2006 and, under the headline Barking Mad, wrote of:

- Dancing lessons for dogs – including 'K9 Freestyle'
- Canine pushchairs for taking dogs on walks without tiring them out
- Dogs riding skateboards
- Pink sheepskin coats for dogs – with matching fleece jackets
- Fur-lined bootees
- Charm collars with diamanté snowflakes, silver fir trees and enamelled Santas (£95)
- 'Happy Woofmas' Christmas stockings.
- 220 gourmet dog treats, including a 30in dried bull's penis

Daily Mail

We all know that the English are big animal lovers. They are also, it seems, lovers of big animals. Figures released by local authorities in 2006 revealed that 12 lions, 14 tigers, 50 leopards and 250 poisonous snakes are among the tally of dangerous wildlife kept in garden

131

sheds and spare rooms across the country. At least 50 members of the crocodile family are in private captivity.

Guardian

Stan Renwick buried his beer-loving pet rat Cyril in a coffin made of beer mats in the grounds of his social club in Barnstaple, Devon.

Sun

Some firms are giving compassionate leave to workers whose pets fall ill or die. The *Independent* on Sunday suggests readers get an ant colony.

Independent

Dennis Bright tamed a robin to eat worms from his mouth. Said Mr. Bright, 59, of Winchester, Hampshire: 'Taming a robin is quite simple. They will sell their soul for a mealworm.'

He calls the robin Cheeky.

Daily Mail

A hungry horse opened the door of a caravan with its teeth after smelling food there. It had to be freed by Hampshire firemen after getting stuck inside.

Sunday Telegraph

Chapter 10

NANNY STATE

After Scotland imposed stringent bans on smoking early in 2006, Glasgow airport – in a caring, sharing way – set aside a small area outdoors where smokers can sit down, flanked by a plastic privet hedge, for a quiet drag. The area quickly became known as 'Benches and Hedges'.

Duncan Campbell, *Guardian*

Barnwell Primary School in Sunderland scrapped its traditional sports day – because it is too competitive.

Sun story carrying the 'You Couldn't Make It Up' tagline.

Another example of Health and Safety Killjoys at work. Two parents were banned from taking their three children into a toddlers' pool at Bridgwater in Somerset. Karen and David Townsend were told their children needed individual supervision.

Mrs Townsend is a lifeguard instructor.

Daily Mail

The clown was dropped from a family fun day at the Bicester in Bloom celebrations because officials thought children would be frightened.

The Times

A man wanting a new phone line is asked if he would like to be ex-directory. 'Yes', he says, and then asks what his new number is going to be. 'We can't tell you that. You're ex-directory. It's data protection. We'll write to you.'

That was in July, reports Terry Wogan in the *Sunday Telegraph* dated 12 November 2006. They still haven't written.

Sunday Telegraph

Amid repeated terrorist alerts in 2006 not all British security arrangements were watertight. Iain Dale in the *Independent on Sunday* reported that at ITN he was told by a security guard to search his own bag, as due to health and safety legislation he wasn't allowed to put his hand in the bag himself.

Independent on Sunday

BBC staff have been stopped from replacing light bulbs because of concerns for health and safety. Instead, the Corporation is paying up to £10 for each replacement bulb to be fitted.

It seems that it takes five people to change a BBC light bulb. Staffers left in the dark would need to find a clerk to get a reference number, then report to a helpline helper. An electrician would ask the store manager for a bulb and then install it.

Sunday Telegraph

In an article headed 'The Death of British Humour – Killed Off By The Forces of Political Correctness', Leo McKinstry repeats a joke about a female Islamic terrorist in a burka. She asks a friend: 'Does my bomb look big in this?'

'Hilarious,' writes McKinsty, 'but is it permissible in cringing modern Britain? Perhaps not.'

Daily Mail

A fire station has been built in Plymouth without the traditional pole because of fears that firemen might get hurt when they reach the ground.

Firefighters were flabbergasted and one said: 'We used to have school visits and let children go down the poles.'

Daily Telegraph

Richard Littlejohn notes that some firemen have been banned from sliding down poles in case they hurt themselves. Also the 'elf and safety nazis' have ruled that it is not safe for them to use stepladders to change smoke alarms. A union official said: 'The use of stepladders contravenes working-at- height regulations.'

Littlejohn comments: 'I suppose rescuing a cat from a tree is out of the question.'

Daily Mail

Paul Wood, of Billingshurst, West Sussex, says that in his newly acquired position as a school caretaker he has had to sign up for 'Ladder Training'. 'The first item on the list of skills I will learn is entitled "What is a ladder?"'

The Times

New Health and Safety Regulations throw up a rich mixture of jobsworths and over-zealous interpretations.

In April 2006 most UK newspapers carried the story of a man being refused permission to carry a tin of paint on a bus in Cardiff. RAF veteran Brian Heale, 73, was ordered off the bus by the driver, who said that his tin of cream emulsion was against new regulations. 'It's crazy,' he said. 'Hysterical. At first I thought the driver was joking. But he parked the bus and called head office. Next thing you won't be able to take a wet umbrella on in case it drips water.'

In fact the bus driver was technically correct. Paint is listed as a hazardous article, but a Cardiff Bus official apologised and admitted there were times when staff needed to display 'a little more flexibility'.

Various newspapers

The Times accompanied the Cardiff bus story with a recent selection of 'Safety First' items:

- In Tewkesbury, Gloucestershire, the meals-on-wheels service was banned from handing out paper napkins because pensioners and the disabled might choke on them.
- At the BBC in Birmingham a woman caught her foot in the revolving doors. The Corporation then issued a memo entitled: 'Revolving Security Door User Instructions', advising staff on how to use a revolving door.
- In Rochdale, police were called to a church to investigate the breaking of a stained glass window. They were unwilling to inspect the damage because 'they did not have specialist ladder training'.
- In Cheltenham, council gardeners were prevented from planting pansies under trees because they risked spraining their wrists trowelling the root-filled soil.

The Times

The villagers of Bromham, near Chippenham, Wiltshire, looked forward to celebrating St George's Day (23 April 2006) – 300 of them planned to tuck into a hearty English breakfast in their community centre. But the charity event was cancelled at the last minute because of a health and safety warning against frying eggs.

The local council's guidelines state that volunteers should not prepare 'protein-based foods without proper training'. Also, the centre did not have the correct facilities to 'chill, prepare and store' the food. So the organisers, who have held fund-raising breakfasts for 15 years, abandoned the event.

Daily Mail

Despite no one ever having been injured during its 25-year existence, Cathedral Camps (in which young people spend their holidays cleaning and maintaining Britain's most important historical buildings) announced in 2006 that it was having to close down because of health and safety regulations.

Earlier in the year the twelfth-century Wymondham Abbey was forced to spend £6,000 on installing a motorised pulley system to light candles on a chandelier after a health and safety adviser decided that standing on a stepladder was too dangerous.

Sunday Telegraph

For over 30 years the lifeboatmen of Lyme Regis raised money during Lifeboat Week by organising Conger Cuddling – knocking volunteers over with a dead conger eel swinging on the end of a rope. The tradition came to an end in 2006 after animal activists complained that it was disrespectful to dead animals.

Daily Express

For more than 100 years the label on Camp Coffee & Chicory showed a Sikh servant standing deferentially at his British master's side serving the coffee from a tray. The 'politically correct' modern version shows the Sikh sitting side by side with his master (a kilted Gordon Highlander officer). They are both enjoying a cup of Camp.

A Racial Equality Council official thought it 'heartening to see that a new message is being sent out.'

David Davidson, Tory MSP, thought it 'political correctness gone mad'.

Daily Mail

Keith Waterhouse was worried about the new Camp label showing officer and servant sipping coffee side by side. What bothered him was how did the drink get to both of them? Who fetched it?

'We are driven to the conclusion that steaming cups of Camp were brought in by another servant, who was then sent about his business, fuming with class resentment.'

Daily Mail

On 18 October 2006 the *Guardian* reported on page three that the Better Regulation Commission thought Britain had become a risk-averse nation that over-protects and over-regulates. National resilience, self-reliance and spirit of adventure could be threatened by a culture that demands the progressive elimination of risk. One expert was quoted as saying: 'We employ health and safety officers to monitor everything we do, from drinking coffee to walking down a hallway.'

But all is not lost. On the same day, the same newspaper, on page seven, reported: 'Egg and spoon races are enjoying a comeback at school sports days.'

Guardian

Members of Ilfracombe Rugby Club in North Devon got a bit fed up with all the health and safety and 'insane red tape' needed to stage a real bonfire in November 2006 – so they staged the world's first virtual bonfire.

An audience of 1,400 turned up to watch a film of a bonfire projected onto a giant screen with sound provided over a PA system. 'It looked a bit like a barn on fire and there wasn't anywhere to bake potatoes – but everybody enjoyed it.'

Western Morning News

Callington Town band in southeast Cornwall were told they could not play Jingle Bells at their Christmas show unless they got a special licence to perform non-religious songs.

Western Morning News

War veterans from the Royal British Legion in Carshalton, Surrey, wanted a flag raised on Remembrance Sunday 2006. Local firemen were happy to go up the 35ft flagpole but a senior officer overruled them, citing health and safety reasons.

The veterans are mostly in their seventies, eighties and nineties, and the local secretary of the Legion, David Plattern, said: 'I thought he was joking at first. It is health and safety madness, just another sign of the barmy society we live in today.'

He had to turn down an offer from 84-year-old Burma veteran Stan Graves who volunteered to climb the flagpole and deliberately get stuck so that when the fire brigade had to rescue him they could fix the flag at the same time.

Daily Telegraph story under the headline
'Up The Pole'

In a story headlined 'It's Not Politically Correct to Say Politically Correct' the *Daily Mail* reported that Kirklees Council in West Yorkshire had produced an Equality Essentials booklet to help train its staff. It told council workers:

- Not to use the phrase 'political correctness' at work in case it offends people
- Not to use words such as 'policeman', 'fireman' and 'chairman' because they are 'exclusionary'
- Not to use 'ethnic' because it is not 'appropriately descriptive'
- Not to move items around on a colleague's desk because it is as bad as punching or kicking them
- After critics called the booklet 'garbage' and 'utterly ridiculous' Richard Light, new Tory leader of the council, said the booklet would no longer be used.

Daily Mail/Yorkshire Post

David Heather, the mayor of Settle and a LibDem councillor on Craven District Council in North Yorkshire, attended the RMT transport union's black and ethnic minority conference in Skipton and assured members that his welcome speech would feature not a single 'coon' joke.

Guardian

A nineteenth-century painting of a monkey playing a violin was removed from an art gallery in Barnsley, Yorkshire, after decades of being on display. There were fears that it could have been offensive and demeaning to animals.

Daily Mail

For six accident-free years, youngsters have enjoyed bobbing up and down in a Postman Pat children's ride outside a shoe shop in St Mary's Place, Market Harborough, Leicestershire. But now Pat's red van has been sent packing by killjoy officials who say it is a hazard – and the shop has been warned for not having a licence and posing a health and safety risk.

Daily Mirror

John Cowper was gobsmacked when a store in York wanted his grandson's hood removed.

The boy was two years old.

Sun

The local fire engine was once the star attraction at many a village fête. But few brigades now allow children to clamber on board. This is to prevent officers who lift children in and out of fire trucks being subjected to false accusations of inappropriate behaviour.

Another reason for the fun-killing decision was given by a Devon Fire and Rescue Service: 'Members of the public may accidentally cause damage that can endanger fire fighters'.

Tory MP Anne Widdecombe deemed the decision: 'Plain stupid'.

Daily Mail

Burnham Grammar School in Buckinghamshire has banned lunchtime football kick-abouts because pupils might get hurt.

Daily Telegraph

In Huddersfield, Yorkshire, a school production of Roald Dahl's *Three Little Pigs* turned the porkers into puppies for fear of upsetting Muslims.

Daily Telegraph

A woman attending a Health and Safety Safer Farming Day in Chester was injured when she fell down an open drain.

A spokesman said: 'It emphasises the need to be vigilant at all times' – rather unfeelingly in the view of Guardian diarist Jon Henley.

Guardian

Chapter 11

FOOD FOR THOUGHT

A St Albans reader of *The Times* wrote: I phoned a restaurant to book a romantic Valentine's dinner and was asked: 'For how many?'

The Times

Robin Kempster, of Brighouse, West Yorkshire, asked for some small eggs in a supermarket and was told: 'They only make them in medium, large and very large these days, sir.'

The Times

You've got to hand it to your British bobby. When nine of them went to Moscow in December 2006 to investigate the poisoning in London of a former Russian spy they left nothing to chance. They took with them Marmite, teabags, marmalade, Lucozade and lots of Cadbury's Crunchie bars.

Sun

Well-padded comedienne Jo Brand had a Q&A session with the *Guardian:*

Q: What foods do you always have in your shopping trolley?

A: Pork pies

Q: Do you take any vitamins or supplements?

A: No. But I have been known to glance at some vegetables or fruit in such a way that they might have believed I was going to eat them in future.

Q: Have you ever dieted?

A: Only in a leap year.

Guardian Weekend Magazine

A reader asked Philip Howard's Modern Times column: 'Which is the correct end to open a boiled egg?'

His reply: 'It doesn't matter a tossed eggshell. What matters is not to spill yolk on your shirt. And to share your toast soldiers with others.'

The Times

Fiona Davies, of Benenden, Kent, spotted this Valentine's Day special offer in a supermarket: 'Delicious crab/prawn delicacies for a romantic meal – Best Before February 11'.

Daily Telegraph

Elizabeth Purslow, of Malmesbury, Wiltshire, remembers being told by her grandmother that the way to a man's heart was through his stomach.

It seems that nothing much changes, because Elizabeth spotted that a speed-dating experiment in April 2006 reported that the best chat-up line of the top-rated female was: 'What's your favourite pizza topping?'

Daily Telegraph

Isabella Martin was seven years old when her parents took her to a restaurant in Cambridge which runs an all-you-can eat deal with children getting their meals for half price. But when the bill came it showed Isabella's meal at the adult price. When challenged staff measured the seven-year-old against a mark on the restaurant wall.

It turned out that Isabella was one centimetre taller than the 1.2m (around 4ft) which was the restaurant's cut off point for cheaper meals.

Daily Mail

Cookery books provide varied answers to the question 'How Do You Make the Perfect Boiled Egg'.

J. B. Hobson, of King's Lynn, Norfolk, told of a Norfolk parson's cook who used to sing Rock of Ages when boiling eggs. 'Three verses for soft-boiled. Five verses for hard-boiled.'

Daily Mail

When it was announced that Tom Cruise planned to eat the placenta after Katie Holmes had given birth to their baby, there was an article by Zoe Williams which started off saying it was an absolutely disgusting idea. But the article ended up giving a recipe for 'Placenta Venetian Style', which involved:

3 mild Spanish onions

1 tbsp of parsley

2 tbsp red wine vinegar

8 thin slices of placenta cut into cubes

Guardian/New Zealand News

All hell was breaking loose in the Middle East. Terrorism was becoming increasingly terrifying. Tony Blair was preparing to pack in the top job.

But in September 2006 what *Independent* readers wanted to let off steam about was... Marmite recipes and the launch of a squeezy plastic-bottle version of the stuff. Hundreds of letters and emails engulfed the newspaper, and mention was made of 'the end of civilisation as we know it'.

The *Independent* responded with an article asking 'What is it about this yeasty, oil-slick gloop that can exhort such extremes of feeling?' Here is some of what they came up with:

- Some cannot live without it. Some would rather eat coal.
- Bill Bryson thought you might have to be British

to appreciate a yeast extract with the visual properties of an industrial lubricant.

- Marmite fans pleaded with Unilever not to go ahead with the plastic squeezy container and one wrote: 'Don't do this. There are few absolutely perfect things in the world, but Marmite, surely, is one of them.'

Independent

It is said of Marmite that you either love or hate it. Artist Dermot Flynn has painted portraits of people – including Margaret Thatcher and chef Gordon Ramsay – using Marmite on toast.

They were displayed at a central London gallery in 2006 and critics said: 'You either love them or hate them.'

The Times

On the same page as the Marmite article the *Independent* addressed itself to another deeply felt issue troubling traditional Britons. 'A whole way of life is at an end,' its columnist John Walsh lamented. 'From next year Smarties will no longer be made in the UK. The flattened-sphere chocs in poster-paint colours will be made in Hamburg. It's outrageous.'

Walsh pointed out that such is the appeal of Smarties that the tubes and their plastic lids were collectors' items. Each plastic lid had a letter on it and gathering all the letters of the alphabet made you an official

Smarties anorak. But last year the cylinders were replaced with a 'hexatube'.

'Honestly, it's like desecrating a stained glass window.'

Independent

Thank goodness that some things never change. The design on Lyle's Golden Syrup tins is Britain's oldest brand – unchanged since 1885 and recognised by 88 per cent of shoppers. Golden Syrup's green and gold tins still show a lion and some bees and the Bible quote that religious Mr Lyle insisted on back in the nineteenth century: 'Out of the strong came forth sweetness.'

Sun/Guinness Book of World Records

In a country that has some of the finest tap water in the world millions of people persist in paying good money for bottled versions which are sometimes not as good.

The *Independent on Sunday* provided a two-page spread on the subject, saying that tap water costs a tiny fraction of bottled water, typically being about a thousandth of the price – averaging £1 per thousand litres. And table water is sometimes no more than repackaged tap water sold in expensive looking bottles.

Independent on Sunday

Classic dishes which used to stiffen the backbone and the upper lip of Britain are set to vanish. A survey of once-popular dishes which are now out of favour included:

- Bath chaps – a West Country delicacy of pigs' cheeks which have been pickled, soaked in water, boiled and then rolled in bread-crumbs: to be eaten cold
- Brawn – jellied pig's head
- Squirrel casserole
- Bedfordshire clanger (scrag end of mutton with kidneys)
- Calf's foot jelly
- Griwel blawd ceirch – oatmeal mixed with gruel

Guardian/Daily Mail

In these days of fast food, there is little wonder that Bath chaps, for instance, are out of favour. Matthew Fort provided a recipe in the *Guardian* which began: 'Cut off pig's cheeks and pickle in brine for two to three weeks. Soak in fresh water overnight. Boil in a cooking bag for three to four hours. Leave to cool in the fridge.'

Guardian

Unhealthy school lunches got plenty of publicity in 2006 and inspired a letter from *Times* reader Alan Cliff, of Rhyl, Denbighshire.

At his grammar school in 1944–54 the salads were always appreciated because many of them contained caterpillars. 'These were carefully removed, lined up on the dinner table and then encouraged to squirm to a winning post. It was the height of cheating to grab an opponent's caterpillar and consume same to prevent victory.'

The Times

Most people lack the discipline to eat healthily – but they are brilliant at coming up with excuses. Researchers identified ten common excuses used to justify consumption of unhealthy food. They included:
- No willpower.
- Too busy – it takes too much time to cook a meal from scratch.
- Healthy food is too expensive.
- Fresh food goes off too quickly and therefore is a waste of money.
- 'There is so much in the news about what is and what isn't good for you that I don't know what I should be buying.'

Daily Telegraph

Following stories that the 'trading standards Gestapo' wanted to ban a Welsh sausage-maker from calling its products Welsh Dragon Sausages (fearing that consumers might think they were buying bangers made from dragon meat), *Times* readers wrote in asking:

- 'Should I be worried about battered fish fingers and frozen cod pieces?' (David Sinclair, Alton, Hampshire).
- 'What is Powys County Council going to do about angel cakes and butterfly buns on sale in Crickhowell?' (Anne Frances, Guildford, Surrey).

The Times

Readers of other papers joined in the fun:
- 'I wonder how much feline content there is in a Lion Bar – and we can only speculate as to the content of spotted dick.' (John Murray, Churchill, Somerset).

Daily Telegraph

Strawberry milkshakes can contain 59 ingredients – none of them strawberry. Among the 59 are: guar gum, cellulose gum, sodium phosphate, seaweed extract, E129 artificial red dye, milk fat and artificial flavour 'as natural as a blue banana'.

Daily Mail

Eliza Smith's cookbook, *The Compleat Housewife* or *Accomplish'd Gentlewoman's Companion*, was first published in 1742 and became a bestseller.

Her cure for a scald mark is: 'Take a pound of hog's lard and two handfuls of sheep dung, boil to an ointment, add a bit of onion and white of an egg. In less than a week it will work well.'

Eliza did not forget the gentlemen and provides this remedy for baldness: 'Take two ounces of boar's grease, one dram of the ashes of burnt bees, one dram of the ashes of Southernwood, one dram of the juice of the white lily root, one dram of oil of sweet almonds and six drams of pure musk and make an ointment of these. And, the day before the full moon, shave the place and anoint it every day with this ointment.'

She was a confident girl, our Eliza, and says of her potions: 'They are all excellent in their kind and have cured when all other means have failed and are ready to serve the publick.'

The Times

Three days later the *Daily Telegraph*'s Judith Wood tried cooking one of Eliza's recipes – Ragout of Pigs' Ears – chosen 'because I know what they look like and so can be certain which end of the animal they come from. I boil them for two hours in one half wine and one half water and the smell is revolting. I fish out the ears, chop them up and add them to melted butter, anchovies, shallots, lemon and mustard. I stir it all up and simmer some more. My ragout is now thick and gloppy and interspersed with pieces of gristle, thick folds of skin and the faintest hint of bristle.'

Her husband arrives home and she whips off the saucepan lid. He wretches and leaves the room. She replaces the lid and they have a fry-up.

Judith says she will keep *The Compleat Housewife* in her kitchen forever, alongside Delia and Jamie, and consult it 'when I urgently have to make a marrow pudding, or pickle broom-buds and especially if I need to dismember a heron.'

Daily Telegraph

Darren Gray was told to remove a flag of St George with the word England on it from the side of his house or face a possible £1,000 fine. Bedford Council said he did not have a licence to advertise.

Darren asked, 'What am I supposed to be advertising?'

'England,' he was told.

Daily Telegraph

Chapter 12

WEDDED BLISS

The *Guardian's Diary* reports: 'Despite this column's well-known aversion to making fun of people's names, we cannot in all conscience move on without informing you that in a charming ceremony at Cockfield church, Ms Kerry Sore and Mr Ben Stiff were declared man and wife.'

Guardian

On the day England won the World Cup in 1966, a lady from Fleet, Hampshire, was in a hospital maternity ward and endured a difficult and long labour. Her husband turned up and asked: 'Did you watch the match?'

Daily Mail

In August 2006 a divorce court awarded a wife £48 million pounds. This reminded Roy Child, of Dorset, of 'the days of comparative sanity' when a judge told a husband:

'Mr Jones, I am going to allow your wife ten shillings a week.'

Mr Jones replied: 'Very good of your honour. I'll try to chip in a bit myself.'

The Times

The Helping Hand Society organised a Swap Social Evening with lady members taking along things they did not need.

Many brought their husbands.

Manchester Evening News item quoted in a 1980s issue of Punch

After reports of 'pre-mooning' (couples celebrating their engagement with an early honeymoon) Martin Murrell, of Rayleigh, Essex, wrote that this was 'what we used to call a dirty weekend'.

The Times

It was pouring with rain the night cyclist Joe Emery of Standlake, Oxfordshire, left a church dance in 1949. He offered the girl with whom he had had the last dance a lift on his crossbar.

'Arriving outside her home,' Mr Emery writes, 'we spent the next half hour beneath a lamppost, in the rain, negotiating her fare.'

They were both soaked when they parted, but now have 55 years of happy married life behind them – and a tandem.

Daily Telegraph

When Tory MP Michael Mates got married for the third time his son James opened his best man's speech with: 'Well, here we all are again.'

Sunday Times

Frank and Anita Milford (98 and 97) celebrated their seventy-eighth wedding anniversary in May 2006 and said that an argument every day is the recipe for a long and happy marriage.

They have had three letters from the Queen and since retiring have taken up gardening, snooker and darts at their nursing home in Plymouth.

Those daily arguments, they say 'come and go, but we are always here for each other'.

The Times/Sun

The seven-year-old marriage of Mr and Mrs Marriage ended in the London Divorce Court on 1 June 2006.

Daily Telegraph

Hilda Dann, 91, has lived all her life in the house where she was born in Ashby, Suffolk. When she married, she and her husband Clifford (also 91) set up home in the same house. In June 2006 they celebrated their platinum (70 years) marriage and said: 'We like it here.'

Sun

A couple were awarded £2,000 because a four-poster bed at a Weston-super-Mare hotel collapsed on their wedding night.

The Times

A passer-by (a jilted lover?) tossed a £500 engagement ring into a busker's collecting bowl in Shrewsbury and said: 'That'll keep you going for a few days.'

Independent on Sunday

Suzanne Cooper, 36, and her husband Michael, of Bristol, were blessed with a baby boy on 06/06/06. He weighed 6lb 6oz and they named him Damien.

The Times/Sun

Anybody who was anybody in politics and the media turned up for the July 2006 wedding of Anji Hunter, old friend and colleague of Tony Blair, and Adam Boulton, political editor of Sky News.

According to one guest, Boulton joked: 'People have made huge efforts to come from all parts of SW1.'

Observer

Harold and Lucy Allgood, of Weymouth, Dorset, both 100 years old, celebrated their seventy-eighth wedding anniversary in July 2006. They attribute their longevity and marriage to tolerance and sea air.

Harold said: 'We fight every day and then make sure we make up afterwards.'

Daily Telegraph

Nicky Heys, a 35-year-old secretary, went into labour three months early and gave birth to a 1lb 12oz boy, Harry, at St Michael's Hospital in Bristol. A few hours after the birth the doctor asked Nicky if she had 'anything to do today'.

'Yes,' said Nicky. 'I've got a wedding to go to. My own.'

Just seven hours after giving birth she discharged herself from hospital at 10am, went to the hairdressers, changed into a spectacular dress and later walked down the aisle. The vicar told the 100 guests what had happened and they burst out clapping.

Nicky and her new husband, Nigel Agar, a 33-year-old flight deck technician, made it through the reception and the speeches and then danced to their favourite song before returning to the hospital to see Harry in his incubator with the bride still in her wedding dress.

Nicky said: 'Everything went exactly as planned – except we had a baby.'

Guardian/Daily Mail

The world's longest-running soap opera had five million devoted Archers' fans gagging for more at the prospect of a spot of adultery. Would Ruth Archer, for 18-years the ever-faithful wife of Ambridge farmer David, go all the way with cowherd Sam?

Cruelly spinning out the storyline until the night of the programme's 15,000th episode (7 November 2006), Ruth and Sam got as far as booking into an Oxford hotel. The *Guardian* covered the affair under the headline: 'Ambridge agog. Would she or wouldn't she?' It said that Middle England had been longing for a knee tremble to rival that of an earlier episode when the village pub landlord had a brief encounter with a barmaid in the shower.

But, at the last minute – the very last trembling minute – Ruth 'keeps her mud-stained overalls' on and decides to unclutch herself from Sam's bosom and flee back to that of her family.

Next day an excited British press gave lashings of coverage with the *Guardian* reporting: 'No consummation. No bouncing on a lascivious bed. Ruth, "having developed a passion for Sam while wiping udders and worrying about TB and mastitis" decided not to let him have his wicked way. What a cop out!'

The *Guardian* gave space on its learned Comment & Debate pages to a leader saying: 'The Archers is, perhaps, the radio equivalent of Marmite... To heathens the cheery tum-te-tum-te-tum-te-tum of the theme tune is enough to cause a stampede for the off switch... There are many others who count The Archers as fundamental to life as mother's milk.'

Guardian

The *Daily Telegraph* also had a leader: 'It provides reassurance that good old-fashioned values still exist. Ruth at last seems to have seen the error of her ways... Listeners should be heartened that her conscience brings her back from the brink... Thankfully, it looks like we are back on solid ground.'

The response of *Daily Telegraph* reader Barry Parkin, of Newton Kyme, North Yorkshire was: 'David Archer gets the short straw. Keeps the whingeing wife and loses his quality cowman.'

Daily Telegraph

Private Eye had its own approach to the 2006 Archers:
Then: Mooo! Baaa! Mooo! Baaa!
Now: Oooh! Aaah! Ooooh! YES!!!
Tum-te-tum-te-tum-te-tum....

Private Eye

Poland has become a favourite stag weekend destination for Scots and the newspaper Dziennik quotes a local saying: 'You can't go round the corner without seeing a Scot showing off what he has under his kilt while one of his mates photographs him. I saw one lying in the gutter with his kilt round his waist. He was drunk and it was freezing. I'm surprised he didn't get frostbite.'

Sun

Chapter 13

WHAT'S UP, DOC?

A 20-year-old man was rushed to hospital after receiving an electric shock. His current condition is not known.
Spotted by Ken Marsh, of Southport, Merseyside, in the
Southport Champion.

Bryan Melvin, of Poole, Dorset, tells of his 11-year-old daughter having a friend whose pregnant mother was overdue. She said that if the baby hadn't arrived by Monday 'the doctor is going to seduce her'.

Daily Mail

Jo Brand jokes about men never being able to understand the pain of childbirth. 'Well,' she says, 'they can if you hit them in the testicles with a cricket bat for 14 hours.'

Observer Magazine

Former *Sun* editor Kelvin MacKenzie tells readers of the Sun that he wrote his 8 March 2007 column from hospital after poisoning himself eating what he thought was an onion but turned out to be a daffodil bulb.

'Don't worry,' he says. 'The doctors say I will be out in the spring.'

Sun

More than 15,000 people were admitted to hospital in 2005–06 after falling out of bed.

Two were admitted after being bitten by a crocodile or alligator.

The Times

An X-ray technician asked a little girl:

'Have you ever broken a bone?'

'Yes,' she replied.

'Did it hurt?'

'No.'

'Really? Which bone did you break?'

'My sister's arm.'

Reported by A. Graber, who overheard the conversation while taking a group of nursery-school kids on a tour of a local hospital.

Reader's Digest

A profoundly deaf woman had an appointment at the audiology department of a hospital in Coventry. After waiting for about an hour she asked how much longer she was going to have to wait. 'Oh,' said the receptionist, 'your appointment has come and gone. The doctor DID call your name.'

Terry Wogan, who signed off his last *Sunday Telegraph* column of 2006 with some of the oddball stories from his readers

Up in Dundee the local NHS has issued an instruction book entitled *Good Defecation Dynamics* which, without putting too fine a point on it, explains how to behave in the bog. Along with a diagram showing how to sit on the throne, there is the following advice:

- Do not slump, but keep the normal curve in your back.
- Place your hands over the lower part of your stomach.
- Keep your mouth open as you bulge and widen.
- Keep your feet well supported – and don't forget to breathe.

The Times, under the headline 'Are You Sitting Comfortably?'

Martin Jones of Eastbourne, East Sussex, wanted *Guardian* readers to know: 'Our primary care trust has a Sexual Health Action Group.'

Guardian

Richard Swann, of Sidmouth, Devon, writes that the NHS advised him in November 2005 that the waiting time for a hearing assessment was between 18 and 22 months – 'but this could be prioritised should I be terminally ill.'

Daily Telegraph

Jockey Wilson Renwick was kicked in the head after a fall from Native Eire and taken to Lancaster Hospital for an X-ray on his left ankle.

Spotted by D. Hanley, of Baydon, Wiltshire, *Racing Post*

To avoid a meeting with his probation officer, James Bunnett, 27, of Norfolk, said he had a hospital appointment. To back this up he changed a hospital letter to his wife – replacing her name with his. Trouble was the letter was from Mrs Bunnett's gynaecologist.

James ended up facing a charge of breaching a community order.

Sunday Times

An executive of Scarborough, Whitby and Ryedale NHS primary care trust said that the closure of a local hospital ward was 'a further demonstration of our ongoing commitment to improving efficiency'.

Whitby Gazette/Guardian

The old adage that tennis elbow takes six months to cure if it is treated and half a year if it is left alone has been borne out by researchers.

The Times

They're old wives' tales – but two-thirds of modern mothers and mothers-to-be believe in some of them according to a survey. They include:

- A baby will be a boy if a wedding ring suspended on a chain above the mother's stomach swings a certain way, if a baby has a slower heart rate or is carried low in the abdomen.
- Of those surveyed, 67 per cent believed that pregnant women need to double their food intake – to 'eat for two'.
- If the mother has frequent heartburn during pregnancy, 55 per cent believed that a baby will be born with lots of hair.
- Commenting on old wives' tales on how to determine the sex of an unborn child, the Royal College of Midwives said: 'Whatever the tale, you have a 50–50 chance of getting it right.'

Daily Telegraph

An 87-year-old woman complained to her doctor about her dentist's quality of treatment. On a subsequent visit to the dentist he extracted two teeth without anaesthetic 'to teach her a lesson'.

He was struck off by the General Dental Council in London.

The Times

A patient in a Devon hospital went to the loo and returned to find her bed occupied by a new admission.

Independent on Sunday

The British Dental Foundation reports flossers cleaning between their teeth with paper clips, matchsticks, nail files, pencils, scissors, knives and screwdrivers.

Sunday Times

'Nurse, the B&Q screwdriver please.' Doctors interrupted surgery to get a £2.50 screwdriver from a Merseyside B&Q store.

A patient was having a metal plate removed, but it had been fitted overseas and none of their NHS screwdrivers fitted.

Daily Telegraph

Chapter 14

DRIVEN TO DISTRACTION

After hackers gained access to the computer controlling the Variable Message Signs in Crawley, Sussex, motorists found themselves being urged to 'F**k Off'.

Daily Telegraph

It is reported that comedian Tommy Cooper sometimes tipped taxi drivers by slipping a rustling item into their breast pockets and saying: 'Have a drink on me.'

The driver would later discover a tea bag.

Sunday Telegraph

Oliver Smith was stopped by the police for driving without a licence, road tax or insurance near his home in Leyland, Lancashire.

Two-year-old Oliver was at the wheel of his battery-powered toy car capable of a top speed of less than 3mph.

The Times

Three of the ladies of the Herstmonceux Women's Institute in East Sussex who campaigned against cars speeding through their village received speeding fines when a camera was introduced.

The Times

In March 2007 the Skoda came top in a list of favourite cars – knocking Japanese models off their perch. The accolade was seen as rehabilitation for a car which had long been the subject of ridicule and a staple for stand-up comics. Some of the cruel jibes included:

- What's a Skoda with twin exhausts called? A wheelbarrow.
- Why do they have rear windscreen wipers? To remove the flies which crash into them.
- Why do they have a rear windscreen heater? To keep people's hands warm when pushing them.
- What information is in a new Skoda's manual? A bus timetable.

Daily Mail

Richard Littlejohn writes in his *Daily Mail* column about a blind Iraqi immigrant convicted of dangerous driving.

Omed Aziz was stopped when police saw his car

swerving all over the road. PC Stuart Edge told Warley magistrates: 'I could see he was blind because he had no eyes.'Aziz also has two fingers missing, is partially deaf and suffers from leg tremors.

He pleaded guilty to driving without a licence, no insurance and no MOT certificate. He was given a three-month suspended prison sentence, had his licence endorsed, was disqualified from driving for three years, and ordered to take an extended driving test and pay £364 costs.

Littlejohn comments: 'How do you endorse the licence of someone who doesn't have one? Why only disqualify him for three years – are they expecting eye surgery to make such leaps and bounds in the next thirty-six months? Who is going to pay his costs? He has no money and lives on incapacity benefit.'

'It's this week's edition of You Couldn't Make It Up', writes Richard.

Daily Mail

In the summer of 2006 there was a growing clamour condemning traffic wardens, local councils and private firms for their punitive parking policies and practices. It may have been coincidence, but hounded motorists could be forgiven for taking some delight in seeing a man with the reputation of being Britain's most notorious wheel clamper being clamped himself.

Gordon Miller returned to his car in Portsmouth to find it immobilised because it had no current tax disc. One of Miller's early victims said: 'This has put a spring in my step.'

Portsmouth Today News / Daily Telegraph

The Morris Minor, ('a poached egg on wheels') which went on sale in 1948, has been voted the most quintessentially British vehicle on the road. It forced the Aston Martin into second place in a survey by the organisers of the British International Motor Show 2006. The Rolls Royce was third, followed by the fire engine, the Mini, black London taxi, double-decker bus, Reliant Robin, milk float and – in at No.10 – the Green Goddess fire engine.

The Times

Perhaps Britain's ferocious traffic wardens could learn a lesson from the Italians.

Peter Rado, of Reading, tells how he parked his car in Rome next to (but not in) a parking space. On returning, he found a printed form in four languages under his wiper. It said: 'Rome, the cherished goal of many international travellers, is very pleased to welcome you. Even the most careful driver can occasionally transgress the local regulations. In this case you have transgressed a parking regulation. However, we are sure that this was unintentional and wish you an enjoyable stay in our city.'

The Times

Coventry Council workmen built a huge £1 million roundabout on the A444 dual carriageway and placed a No Exit sign before every turn off.

Motorists following the instructions ended up going round in circles, causing traffic chaos – but such is the polite demeanour of British drivers that no one complained for five weeks.

Coventry Telegraph

There was a clutch of letters in *The Times* about the delights of the tiny Bond Minicar three-wheeler.

Kelvin Chapman, of Bingley, West Yorkshire, remembered how, in the 1950s, their Labrador used to sleep in the village road. A Bond Minicar once ran into the Lab. Having been rudely awakened the dog stood up – and turned the car over, complete with driver.

The Times

Another Bond Minicar letter came from Eric Dehn, of Bristol. He tells of keeping a record of any moving vehicle 'triumphantly passed by ours'. He also recalls being overtaken by a nun on a motorised bicycle, but rejoices in 'eighty-one miles to the gallon. Happy Days.'

The Times

Lorry driver Patrick van Houdt was delivering a load of coke to an iron foundry in Wadebridge, Cornwall, when he lost his way. He drove his 7.5-tonne rig into a residential cul-de-sac, tore his way through two trees and smashed into several cars.

The owner of one of the cars told him: 'If I had a gun I'd shoot you.'

Van-Houdt replied: 'Lady, if I had a gun I'd shoot myself.'

Guardian

A driver who ignored No Parking signs returned to find his car blocked in by scaffolding. He had left his Renault Clio in Totnes, Devon, where builders were due to start work – which meant putting poles in front and behind the Clio, pinning it in.

Sun

A coach driver relied on his sat-nav when taking schoolchildren on a trip to the 500-year-old Hampton Court, the opulent Tudor residence of Henry VIII, a palace which nestles in 750 acres of lavish grounds.

They spent four hours lost in London before turning up at Hampton Court – a tiny side street in North London.

The coach firm has now told its drivers to use maps and an AA spokesman said: 'If you tap rubbish into your sat-nav, you get rubbish out.'

The Times

The Times embellished its Hampton Court story with other sat-nav blunders:

- An ambulance followed sat-nav instructions for what should have been a 20-minute journey transferring a patient between Ilford and Brentwood. The patient survived a 400-mile round trip via Manchester.
- A Four Tops tribute band missed a sold-out concert after confusing Cheltenham with Chelmsford.
- A woman dodged oncoming traffic for 14 miles after misreading her sat-nav system and went the wrong way up a dual carriageway. Police said it was a miracle that nobody was hurt on the A3(M) Portsmouth to London road.

The Times

English lambs were clipped to look like poodles and sold at high prices to rich Japanese.

The scam was rumbled when a Japanese movie star complained that her poodle refused to bark or eat dog food.

Sunday Times

Chapter 15

NOT DEAD, JUST RESTING

A lady who died wanted her ashes scattered over Harrods to make sure that her daughter visited her at least twice a week.

Financial Times

Courses on how to help people who are contemplating suicide are to be held in Llandrindod.

Mid-Wales Journal

Two women went to view the open coffin of a friend and one said: 'She looks wonderful. Why, she looks better than I do.'

The other replied: 'You're right. But remember, you've got flu.'

Sarah Short, *Reader's Digest*

'Always Look on the Bright Side of Life' is the second most popular song at funerals.

Mail on Sunday

Professor Richard Wiseman of the University of Hertfordshire, investigating the psychology of humour, revealed that Spike Milligan was the author of the world's funniest joke:

A man finds a friend lying dead and phones the emergency services.

'My friend is dead. What can I do?'

'Calm down, sir. First, let's make sure he's dead.'

There is a silence and then a gunshot is heard. Back on the phone the man says:

'OK. Now what?

Daily Telegraph

Bob Wysome, of Wellington, Shropshire, writes about the time he was organist at a Scottish funeral and played *Fantasy on a Scottish Folk Tune*.

Afterwards a Scottish mourner expressed his appreciation of the playing of a national tune. 'However,' said the mourner, 'it would perhaps be better next time if you chose something other than *Will Ye No' Come Back Again*.'

The Times

Has *Times* reader Jim Platt-Higgins, of Purley, Surrey, hit on the secret of everlasting life?

He says that he has read that, statistically, one is unlikely to die within a year of making a will. 'I update mine annually and the theory has worked well so far.'

The Times

P. Mary Ogle, of London NW, got plenty of birthday cards wishing her 'many happy returns of the day'. But the card which records her membership of the Royal Horticultural Society was less optimistic, stating 'Life Member' and 'Expires end November 2006.'

The Times

Lesley McGuinness's husband was a devoted Newcastle United fan. When he died she had created for him a solid granite tombstone in the shape of a footballer's shirt in the Toon's black and white stripes. The inscription says simply: 'DAD 1'. The grave's flower vase is a model of a black and white football and the whole creation won the gravestone industry's award for Most Original Memorial of the Year.

Monumental mason Simon Richard said: 'Football is a religion in Newcastle. I sell more gravestones with footballs on them than with Jesus.'

The Times

The footballer's grave story was accompanied by some classic tombstone epitaphs:

- Here lies the body of Jonathan Blake.
  Stepped on the gas instead of the brake.
- The children of Israel wanted bread and the Lord sent them manna. Old Wallace wanted a wife and the Devil sent him Anna.
- Here lieth W.W. who never more will trouble you, trouble you.
- Here lies Ezekial Aikle, aged 102. The good die young.

The Times

Seen on a door at Peterborough Crematorium:
PLEASE DO NOT USE THIS ROOM TO WAIT FOR YOUR FUNERAL
Spotted by S. Stevens of Peterborough, *Daily Mail*

A *Times* reader reveals that after paying the final electricity bill when his mother died the local electricity people sent a letter saying that they could provide all her requirements at her new address.

The Times

This was followed by a man from Westcliff on Sea, Essex, who tells of a letter from British Gas: 'Dear Mrs Pack (deceased), Can you please explain the reason for failing to pay your most recent bill?'

The Times

Vic Fearn & Co, coffin-makers in Nottingham, build 'crazy coffins'. They have built them for customers who wanted to be buried in:

- A Rolls Royce
- An aeroplane
- A Ferrari
- An electric guitar

'It is rather a niche business,' they say.

The Times

'I may not have succeeded in halting the war, but I did secure the right of Parliament to decide on war.' This epitaph referring to war in Iraq is on the tombstone of parliamentarian Robin Cook and inspired the *Guardian*'s *G2* magazine to dig up some others:

- 'Life is a jest and all things show it. I thought so once and now I know it' – screenwriter Robert Keats
- 'That's all folks' – Mel Blanc, the voice of Bugs Bunny
- 'Excuse me, I can't stand up' – Groucho Marx.
- 'I told you I was ill' – Spike Milligan.
- The epitaph Winston Churchill suggested for himself was:
- 'I am ready to meet my Maker. Whether my Maker is prepared for the great ordeal of meeting me is another matter.' Sadly it never made his tomb.

Guardian G2

Plymouth Argyle football fans can have a personalised funeral service with their coffins decked in the club's green and black colours – and the chance of having the wake at the Home Park ground.

Daily Telegraph

Chapter 16

TRANSPORTS OF DELIGHT

Announcement on a Hastings to London train: 'Please mind the gap between the timetable and reality.'

Financial Times

David Drew, Labour MP for Stroud in Gloucestershire, missed a Parliamentary debate on the failings of First Great Western Trains.

He was late because his First Great Western train was behind schedule.

Sun

Railway punctuality is a favourite subject for readers' letters and Mike Lowry of Middle Coombe, near Shaftesbury, Dorset, came up with a classic.

He had missed a 10pm train at Delhi in 1943, but the

assistant station manager comforted him with: 'You lucky man, sahib. Yesterday's 10 o'clock train will be here in 15 minutes.'

The Times

The late musician Dennis Brain is said to have asked a fellow train passenger to turn off his radio. His request was refused – so he took out his French horn and started to play.

Ron Sloggett, Fleet, Hampshire, *Daily Telegraph*

Some genuine complaints made to UK holiday companies:

- No one told us there would be fish in the sea. The children were startled.
- My fiancé and I booked a twin-bedded room but were placed in a double-bedded room. We hold you responsible for the fact that I find myself pregnant.
- It took us nine hours to fly to Jamaica from England. It took the Americans only three hours.
- And, from a holidaymaker who chose Spain: 'There were too many Spanish people. The food is Spanish. Too many foreigners.'

Reader's Digest

David Jager, 42, spent an hour waiting for a bus in Penzance and got so fed up he stole one and tried to drive himself home.

He crashed into a kerb and later told police: 'I have done something stupid.'

Western Morning News

Scene: Bali airport. A group of British holidaymakers are separated into men and women and put into different rooms. Five girls are strip-searched and one of them says afterwards to the men:

'The only thing that got us through that was thinking of you going through the same thing.'

'But we didn't', says one of them.

'Oh', says Kate Moss.

Hugo Rifkind's People column, *The Times*.

When the international jet-set chat about the fun spots of the Western world it is fair to assume that Newport does not crop up in their conversation very often.

K. Watkins in the *South Wales Argus*, quoted in an old copy of *Punch*

Roz Gordon from Suffolk completed the 1,162 miles from John o' Groats to Lands End using seventy-three types of transport including a pogo stick, Space Hopper, luggage trolley, stilts, catamaran, stretcher, wheelbarrow, rickshaw, dog-sled, skateboard and a piggyback from her brother. It took her six weeks.

Independent on Sunday

Harrow commuters who use the Metropolitan Line were concerned about possible cuts in the service – and were reported to be outraged that 30 per cent of seats could be slashed.

Spotted by Ian Andrews, *Harrow Observer*

The next time your train is late take some small comfort from the early days of railways when some companies objected to the publication of timetables. They feared the tables would make punctuality 'a sort of obligation'.

Leo McInstry in the *Mail on Sunday* comments: 'It's a line some of our current operators would no doubt like to borrow.'

Mail on Sunday

Eccles in Lancashire has a state-of-the-art bus shelter that cost an astonishing £250,000 and is so grand that it is called 'A Passenger Waiting Environment'.

A slight drawback, passengers complain, is that it is not at the point where buses actually stop.

Daily Mail

Commuter Paul Bartlett, of Thorndon, Suffolk, won a battle with rail operator One, which wanted to charge him £1.95 for a cup of hot water to pour onto his herbal tea bag.

He pointed out that the firm's coffee cost only £1.50 and the train company slashed the price of hot water to 10p.

Daily Telegraph

Items left behind on London's public transport have included:

- A park bench
- A grandfather clock
- A bishop's crook
- A stuffed eagle complete with a half eaten pigeon in its mouth
- A do-it-yourself vasectomy kit
- A pair of breast implants
- A jar of bull's sperm

Guardian G2

A superfast Pendolina train run by Virgin pulled to a stop in Rugby and passengers were astonished to hear this announcement: 'If anyone has some nuts and bolts will they please come forward.'

The blades on the train's windscreen wipers were loose and the train could not proceed without them. But, unsurprisingly, no passenger could produce the necessary nuts and bolts so 500 of them had to disembark and squeeze onto the next train.

Daily Telegraph

The ever-helpful National Rail Enquiries website spells out some of its definitions in commendably clear-cut language. It explains that:

- DELAYED means 'This service is delayed.'
- CANCELLED means 'This service has been cancelled.'

- ON TIME means 'This service is on time.'
- NO REPORT means 'There is no report on the progress of this service yet.'

Sunday Telegraph

The Queen and Prince Philip took the 5pm commuter train from Liverpool Street Station on Thursday 23 November 2006 to spend the weekend in Suffolk. Passengers found themselves in the same carriage as the Monarch and her husband. Regular commuters may have noticed some slight differences from their daily routine:

- As a treat a steward appeared and served the royal couple shortbread biscuits and tea in china cups.
- The royals travelled with ten members of their staff and security personnel.
- The train company graciously waived the two £46 first-class fares for a single to Ipswich.
- The train arrived at Ipswich three minutes early.

Most recognised their distinguished travelling companions and some took mobile phone pictures when they alighted with other passengers. But one lady was heard to say: 'I'm sure that lady is on the television.'

Daily Telegraph/Sun

Tory leader David Cameron discovered that he had lost his ticket when he got off a Tube train at Wembley Park. He told Underground staff: 'I can assure you that I did buy one.'

A member of staff said: 'Surely in your line of work, you would have the money to buy a second ticket?'

'Yes,' Cameron replied, 'but there's not much security in my line of work you know.'

He was then asked to pay £3 for another ticket – avoiding a £30 fine. Later on he found his ticket.

Sunday Telegraph/Daily Mail

The *Sunday Telegraph*'s Nigel Farndale was travelling on South West Trains when this announcement was made: 'We regret to inform you that the buffet trolley is unable to come down the train as it is too wide for the aisles.'

Think about it, he writes. Were trolleys made to the wrong specifications, but sent out anyway in the hope that no one would notice?

Sunday Telegraph

Unhappy commuters handed in fake railway tickets in a protest at service cuts and overcrowded trains on First Great Western. The tickets read:

- Worst Late Western
- Ticket Type – Standing Only
- Class – Cattle Truck
- Price – UP 12 per cent
- Route – Hell & Back

One commuter protested about having to travel in a lavatory with two other passengers.

Daily Telegraph

The Times called the Great Western rebellion 'a very British protest' and compared it with the time when villagers were upset about the threatened closure of their local school in Lanreath, Cornwall.

The protesters travelled to London and turned a patch of grass into the site of a Women's Institute tea party, complete with Morris dancers and a flock of sheep.

The Times

In February 2007 British Airways said it was going to charge £120 for additional suitcases put into the hold.

Alison Opie, of Rodmersham Green, Kent, wrote: 'I take two suitcases on long-haul flights so that I have spare clothes available should the airline lose one of them. BA's record on lost luggage is, I believe, rather poor.'

Daily Telegraph

VisitBritain, the official website guide for visitors to these islands, has compiled some of the daftest questions asked at its tourist information offices:

- Is Wales closed during the winter?
- Which Tube line goes to Edinburgh?
- Why on earth did they build Windsor Castle on the flight path to Heathrow?
- Who feeds the Loch Ness monster?

Reader's Digest

Mike Coster, of Sidcup, Kent, remembers putting his shoes outside his door for overnight cleaning at a very good hotel in Perth, Australia.

Next morning he found this note inside one of the shoes: 'You are in Australia now. Clean your own.'

Daily Telegraph

Writing in the *Telegraph* the following day, Gordon Simpson, of Bournemouth, pointed out that Mr Coster was lucky.

'I was flying as aircrew to Australia and my captain left his shoes outside his hotel room. In the morning they had gone and had been replaced by a note: 'Thanks for the shoes. They are too big for me, but I am sure they will fit my brother.'

Daily Telegraph

Dylan Thomas described Laugharne as the strangest town in Wales. George Tremlett, legendary owner of the local bookshop is a great source of stories. He tells of the Laugharne farmer who boarded a bus along with a pig. He asked for one return ticket and one single ticket to St Clears' abattoir.

Guardian (Travel Section)

Douglas MacDonald of Norwich remembers Americans being puzzled by posters proclaiming: 'Enjoy the Norfolk Broads'.

The Times

Chapter 17

WHAT'S IN A NAME?

Mr Rick Shaw is a spokesman for the Cumbria Ambulance Service.

Guardian

Anxious mother overheard in a Glasgow department store: 'Pandora, come away from that box.'

Financial Times

The surname Cock is most common in Truro and Smellies are likely to come from Glasgow. Nutters turn up in Blackburn and Piggs in Newcastle.

A survey from the University of Central London found that eccentric appellations are often the products of specific towns and cities – with Strangers turning up in Torquay and Dafts in Nottingham.

Daily Mail

YOU CERTAINLY COULDN'T MAKE IT UP

The following were submitted by *Telegraph* readers:

- Dave Little, of Richmond, Yorkshire, noted – in the heart of Herriot Country – a fast food outlet called All Pizzas Great and Small.
- David Lord, of Keighley, West Yorkshire, has his lawn mowed by a young man trading as 'Lawnorder'.
- Brian Howard of Enfield, Middlesex tells of a baker who advertised 'slightly imperfect Maids of Honour'.
- Julian Clapp, of Shoscombe, Somerset, writes of 'William the Concreter' delivering ready-mixed concrete in the Battle area.
- There is also a 'Jim'll Mix It' in Essex.

Daily Telegraph

Tim Sugg, of Hope Valley, Derbyshire, saw a van in Bradford carrying the message: 'Khan and Khan – Builders. You've tried the cowboys – now try the Indians.'

Daily Telegraph

Anthony Bennett, of Bridport, Dorset, found a Lyme Regis chimney sweep – Alexander the Grate.

Daily Telegraph

Rachel and Phil Gould, of Barnardiston, Suffolk, had their house extended by Complete Fabrications.

Daily Telegraph

A *Daily Telegraph* reader from Tiverton, Devon, spotted a trailer café in a layby on the A38 called Breakfast at Timothy's.

Daily Telegraph

Emma Fawkes, of Oxford, came across Junk and Disorderly – a second-hand furniture shop in West London.

Daily Telegraph

Guy Arnoux, of Wells, Somerset, once dealt with solicitors in Ireland called Crooks and Phibs.

Daily Telegraph

Ashley Truluck, of Broad Chalke, Wiltshire, found a South London shop having a 'Massive Shoe Sale. Buy one, get one free.'

Daily Telegraph

David Dent, of Northwich, Cheshire, remembers the Bronte Balti in Howarth, Yorkshire.

Daily Telegraph

Paul Gray, of Sandhurst, Berkshire, became fond of a Birmingham Indian restaurant called Shirley Temple.

Daily Telegraph

Newspaper columnists poked fun at people who named their children after modern celebrities, but Lucinda Ganderton, of Richmond, Surrey, pointed out that the 1871 census for England includes:

- 1967 Elizabeth Bennetts
- 46 Horatio Nelsons
- 23 Percy Shelleys

These were joined in 1881 by:

- 2 Oliver Twists, and
- 2 Bill Sykes

The Times

It was the ultimate in Keeping up with the Joneses – 1,224 individuals arrived in Cardiff in November 2006 to establish a record for the largest gathering of people with the same surname. They came from as far away as Australia and America and included people like Arwel Jones, of Llanrwst, North Wales – a butcher who has more than 400 customers called Jones.

Singer Tom Jones couldn't make it and perhaps it was just as well. Purists know that his real name is Woodward.

The Sunday Telegraph enjoyed making a strapline out of a question posed by a cab driver who, on turning up at the do, asked: 'Anybody here ordered a taxi in the name of Jones?

Sunday Telegraph

The Times Book of Names was published in January 2007. It analysed the most popular first names and carried a leader on the subject headlined:

'Today Every Tom, Dick and Harry Is Called Maximus Peaches Zorro'.

The Times

Jon Henley insists that the Diary he writes for the *Guardian* is not interested in making fun out of people's names – but readers keep sending them in, for example:

- Dentith and Dentith is the name of a dental practice in Oakham, Rutland.
- Doolittle and Doolittle are a Kidderminster estate agency.
- A key member of The Urology Team in Austin, Texas, is Dr Dick Chopp.
- At the Manchester Evening News one of the staff is Mr Wayne Ankers.
- The man at Passengerfocus who handles complaints about train services is Ashley Grumble.
- Anyone contacting St Alban's district council for advice on trees is likely to speak to Andrew Branch.

Guardian

Seen outside Cromer High School by John Wilkinson of Kidderminster, Worcester

Daily Mail

Chapter 18

RAISE YOUR GLASSES

A. Ghillie from Speyside poses the question: 'If whisky be the water of life then why am I lying here?'

Sunday Telegraph

A national poll reveals that one third of British men have a beer gut— what's more seven per cent of those polled expressed pride at having one.

Independent on Sunday

On New Year's Day 2007 it seemed appropriate that the *Independent* should have a leader on hangovers. It came up with 'this cheery thought':

'There is no such thing as a hangover cure... As Francis Bacon once put it: "I have never found any panacea for a hangover. I don't think one exists, apart from suicide."'

Independent

Patsy Cole, of Salisbury, Wiltshire, and a friend went to a village fête dressed as Sooty and Sweep. They were playing with children at the fête when one boy said to her: 'You've been drinking... You smell just like my mum.'

Daily Mail

Fame doesn't come easy. Barmaid Mairi Duncan was known to the locals at the Unicorn in Dalkeith, Midlothian, but her fame didn't spread much further – until she plunged 14ft through the trapdoor behind the bar.

Video footage of her fall first appeared on ITV's *You've Been Framed* and was picked up by the video-sharing website YouTube. She was then invited to Hollywood to appear on Jimmy Kimnel Live, and the footage of her disappearing down into the cellar became one of YouTube's most popular videos.

Daily Telegraph

More than five million Britons admit to buying £1 billion worth of stolen goods in pubs, according to a Halifax Home Insurance survey.

Daily Mail

One of the safest sporting bets is Germany to beat England in the World Marbles Championships held every year at the Greyhound pub at Tinsley Green, West Sussex.

It's a question of attitude. The Germans take it

seriously and go into training days ahead of the match. The British attitude is summed up by the name of one of its teams: 'Only Here for the Beer', and they stick strictly to the rule that pints must be consumed at all times.

An official of the British Marbles Board of Control explained: 'The winners get a silver trophy and the runners-up get a crate of beer. You'd have to be mad to want to come first. Or German.'

Guardian

The *Daily Telegraph* sent a lucky reporter to taste some whisky at the Scotch Malt Whisky Society. He was able to shatter some of the myths that whisky bores have clung to down the ages:

- The right type of glass is not the standard cut-glass whisky tumbler. The glass used in the industry – the nosing glass – is tulip-shaped like a sherry glass, with a narrow mouth that helps contain the aroma.
- Hold the glass by the stem to avoid warming the liquid.
- You should also add water to halve the alcoholic strength to around 20 per cent alcohol-by-volume. This may not be popular with those who do not approve of adding water, but it is essential if you wish to avoid anaesthetising your taste buds.
- Take a generous sip. Is it smooth, creamy, oily or spirity?

- Move the whisky around your mouth, checking the balance of sweet, sour, salty and bitter sensations.
- Note how long the flavours linger and what you taste after the whisky has gone.
- Repeat the process as long as you are still making sense.

Daily Telegraph

A news story in April 2006 about a ban stopping Indian distillers putting 'Scotch' labels on their bottles reminded John Johnson, of Bexhill-on-Sea, of a conversation overheard on a train some 30 years ago.

It was all about a bottle of whisky seen behind the bar of a Delhi hotel with a label reading: 'Queen George IV Whisky. Distilled from genuine Scottish grapes.'

The Times

Next day a *Times* letter revealed that the label described above went on to say that the 'Scottish grapes' were 'pressed in the cellars of Buckingham Palace.'

Submitted by Mark Thompson, Selby, North Yorkshire, *The Times*

What's really in your pint, asked the *Guardian* in May 2006. The answer makes for grim reading, and includes:

- The ground air bladders of fishes (for fining)

- Seaweed extract
- Sulphur
- Ascorbic acid
- Caramel (for colour)
- Betaglucamate (to accelerate brewing)
- Enzyme (to assist the yeasts)
- Salts and minerals (to correct the brewing water)

A now-defunct Hull brewery was said to cure sides of ham in the brewing beer, and another delightful old chestnut concerns this or that brewer who would gauge his beer ready when the dead rats floated to the top of the fermentation tank.

Guardian

While holidaying in Winchester, Geoff Wright, of Doncaster, South Yorkshire, was pleased by 'the number of sensible pubs that allowed well-behaved dogs, but not children'.

Daily Telegraph

In June 2006 a small treeless island off the coast of Barrow-in-Furness advertised for a king. It is made clear that the monarchy can be claimed only by someone qualified to run a pub.

The honorary title of King of Piel Island has been given to the landlord of the Ship Inn since it was built in 1836 – the only pub on the 20-acre island. Piel is not a bountiful kingdom. There is a fourteenth-century castle, six holiday cottages and a seal colony.

The *Times*, under the headline 'King Wanted: Must Be Able to Serve Full English Breakfast'

The Swan at Little Totham, Essex, gets into the Best Pub lists and one of them says: 'An unashamedly beer-centric village pub. Real ale types will find much to love – including house rules that forbid swearing, singlets and caps put on backwards.

Observer

The *Sun* referred to the 'notoriously boozy' reputation of union dinners at TUC conferences and claimed: 'Invitations tend to say '6 for 9.30'.

Sun

The English pub, one of our great gifts to civilisation, is in mortal danger, wrote Michael Henderson. They are closing down in the towns as well as in rural areas. Even when they survive their character is threatened by the rise of the gastro pub and the march of the voracious chains, neither of which place much emphasis on the quirky or the particular which lies at the heart of what makes a pub a pub.

For the pub, the local, the boozer, is such an extraordinary English (not British) institution that it cannot simply be wished into existence.

Good pubs are shaped by local forces and by the

people who use them. They are not necessarily for the benefit of outsiders, who should not feel threatened if they are welcomed less warmly than they might like, though there is no excuse for surly behaviour.

Daily Telegraph

On the same page of the *Telegraph*, reader Julian Brownridge, of Rochester, Kent, remembered how, many years ago, Hilaire Belloc wrote: 'When you have lost your inns, drown your empty selves, for you will have lost the last of England.'

Daily Telegraph

Hampshire bell ringers have completed their mission to visit all 750 pubs in Britain with the word 'Bell' in their names.

Independent on Sunday

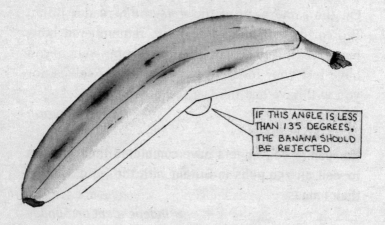

IF THIS ANGLE IS LESS THAN 135 DEGREES, THE BANANA SHOULD BE REJECTED

The Times Cut Out and Keep Guide to the perfect EU banana was published under the headline WHY IS THIS BANANA LEGALLY CURVED INSTEAD OF JUST CROOKED? BECAUSE IT IS THE FRUIT OF THE FINEST JUDICIAL MINDS IN EUROPE.

Under EU Regulation 2257/94 bananas are required to be at least 5.5inches long and 1.06inches round and to not have 'abnormal curvature' – as set out in an eight page directive.

Chapter 19

SCHOOL'S OUT

Amid a flurry of letters about institutions offering bogus university degrees, a correspondent told *The Times* about his BA in Ugandan studies, which he acquired for £10 via the small ads in *Private Eye*.

'It is personally signed by Idi Amin, King of Scotland, so there can be no doubt about its authenticity.'

Submitted by Adam Craig, BA (University of Kampala)
Gibraltar, *The Times*

Joyce Reece, of Northampton, has a friend whose five-year-old daughter was asked at her new school:
'What is your father's name?'
'Dad', she replied.
'But what does your Mummy call Daddy?'
'Baldy', was the answer.

Daily Mail

St Hilda's, the last remaining all-women's Oxford University college (whose students are affectionately known as Hildabeasts) decided in June 2006 to end their 113-year-old ban on male students.

Those who voted in favour of change said it was time that the college – nicknamed 'the Virgin Megastore' – shook off its image as a sanctuary for lesbians and nymphomaniacs.

Daily Telegraph

An educational publication aimed at making Shakespeare more accessible to modern pupils has boiled down the balcony scene in Romeo and Juliet to:

Girl: What are you thinking about?

Boy: Oh, just moons and spoons in June.

Girl: Wow. Give us a snog then.

The Times

A citizenship guide used in thousands of schools describes cross-country running as a form of physical abuse.

The guide describes how human rights legislation affects pupils' lives and tells them: 'You have the right to be protected from emotional or physical abuse' and gives bullying and cross-country as examples.

Sunday Telegraph

Southfields Community College in Wandsworth, London, lays claim to being the most cosmopolitan in Europe. Its pupils speak 71 languages.

The Times

Oxbridge has become famous for throwing oddball questions into interviews with students. (Such as: 'Tell me about a banana'.) But gone are the days of the Cambridge tutor who was said to hurl a rugby ball at interviewees. If they dropped it they were out. If they caught it they were in. If they drop-kicked it through the window they got a scholarship.

Daily Telegraph

Brasenose College, Oxford, had similarly distinctive admission procedures. Between the wars principal Dr W.T.S. Stalybrass would fling a rugby ball at applicants. Those who caught it were admitted.

Daily Mail

Oddball Oxbridge questions were back in the news in October 2006 when the following were some of the examples quoted:
- **What is the percentage of the world's water contained in the average cow?**
- **Put a monetary value on this teapot.**
- **Here is a piece of bark. Please talk about it.**
- **Describe a potato, then compare it with an onion.**

• Are you cool?

Oxbridge Applications, a company which offers prospective students help, said: 'The interview process is notoriously eccentric. It is one way of finding out who cuts the mustard.'

Guardian / The Times

Some children living in urban areas believe that cows lay eggs and that bacon comes from sheep, says a study by Dairy Farmers of Britain.

Western Morning News

Chapter 20

PLAIN ECCENTRIC

Elvis Presley impersonator Geraint Benney of Aberdare says he has been getting death threats because he is bald.

Fans complain that he shows disrespect, but Geraint says being bald makes him stand out.

Sun/Sunday Times

The Duke of Marlborough is reported as having confronted an interested onlooker in the urinals of his gentleman's club with: 'Take a good look. There are only 24 of these in the country.'

Observer

Keith Waterhouse vividly remembers the late Jeffery Bernard, the serious Soho drinker-about-town, pointing out that your average betting shop has three or four Paying In windows but only one Paying Out window.

He remained a gambling addict.

Daily Mail

Gilbert Beale, an eccentric who left an indelible mark on the Berkshire countryside, had a passion for peacocks. His favourite peahen, Laura, used to ride with him when he toured his estate in his Rolls Royce.

Henley Life magazine

In November 2006 Cherie Blair received the Freedom of the City of London, which entitles her to herd sheep over London Bridge, carry a drawn sword and be drunk and disorderly without fear of arrest.

The Times

Anthony Willoughby, 56, a founder member of the Cock Up Club, qualified for membership by taking an expedition into the Papua New Guinea jungle with twenty-four bottles of wine, but no food.

The club was founded in the Folly Wine Bar in Petersfield, Hampshire, and Willoughby says: 'Most of the best cock-ups come from trying to impress women'.

Jeannie M. Gallagher wrote asking if her husband's

214

greatest achievement qualifies him for membership of the Cock Up Club. 'After all, not many people throw a coin into Rome's Trevi Fountain and miss!'

Sunday Telegraph

In October 2006 Victoria Hughes became the first professional lavatory attendant to make it into the Oxford Dictionary of National Biography – that leviathan of British heroes and eccentrics.

Mrs Hughes kept notes of surprising encounters in the Ladies from 1929 to 1962 and was glad of her starting salary of 4s 6d for looking after a loo near the Clifton Suspension Bridge.

The kettle was always on and she dispensed tea and sympathy and showed compassion to those of her customers who were prostitutes. 'They gave me a sort of companionship and warmth,' she wrote.

Daily Telegraph

Victoria joins other ODNB eccentrics such as Henry Moat (1871–1940) 'an enormous purple man – like a benevolent hippopotamus with a voice like a foghorn'.

Henry was the colourful valet of Sir George-Sitwell, and he would carry behind his master a large inflatable cushion when Sitwell was making his way to obscure research in the British Museum. One of Sir George's ideas was that knife handles could be made of a substance derived from condensed milk, to which the admirable valet responded: 'Yes, Sir, but what if the cat gets them?'

Moat brought with him a pet seal with which he travelled by train from his native Whitby.

Daily Telegraph

A reader wrote to the *Daily Telegraph* wondering if there was a Society of People Who Have Not Seen the Sound of Music and Have No Intention of Doing So.

This was followed by:

- 'I have formed the Society of People Who Have Never Seen a Single Episode of Coronation Street or EastEnders and Have No Intention of Doing So.' Patrick O'Sullivan, Tunstall, Sunderland
- 'Is there anyone who would like to join the Society of People Who Refuse to Shop at Tesco?' C. Barry-Walsh, London NW6
- 'I belong to the Refined Society of People Who Have Never Attended a Car Boot Sale.' Margaret Powling, Paington, Devon
- Alan Whitefield, of Milton Keynes, said he was not only fully qualified to join the Sound of Music society mentioned above, but also the Society for Those Who Have Never Read Harry Potter and the Society of People Who Have Never Been to IKEA.
- Chris Swindin, of Filey, North Yorkshire reported being a traumatised member of the Society of

People Who Wish They Had Never Been to IKEA.

- **Peter Tuthill, of Abu Dhabi, wondered if there would be any interest in forming a Society of People Who Have Neither Eaten at McDonald's nor Kentucky Fried Chicken.**

Daily Telegraph

The response to the above was so big that it became a sort of national game. Radio 4's *Today* presenter John Humphrys told listeners that he had never bought a lottery ticket. John Mortimer said he would most avoid the Society of Hobbit Lovers – and the *Daily Telegraph* was inspired to launch 'The Society of People Who Have Never'.

Early members included rebels who say No to Ikea, iPods, Pot Noodles, the Mousetrap, baseball caps, mobile phones, discos in Ibiza, body piercing, anything with the word Celebrity in the title, PlayStations, Disneyland, Legoland, Alton Towers, folk dancing, the Beatles, Jamie Oliver recipes, TV, Sudoku, bottled water, James Bond movies, potato skins and chicken in a bucket. One reader fancied a Society of People Who Have Never Heard of David Beckham. Another had never seen Blue Peter and asked: 'Do I get a badge?'

Daily Telegraph

It all got too much for some readers. Alan Henbest, of Bourne End, Buckinghamshire, wrote of 'silly letters cluttering up' his newspaper and said he would consider joining the Society For Those Who Stopped Reading the *Telegraph* in Disgust.

Daily Telegraph

The *Guardian*'s Diary launched 'an enthralling hunt' for Britain's Most Exciting Museum, and entries considered included:
- The Dog Collar Museum at Leeds Castle
- The Savings Bank Museum of Ruthwell, Dumfries
- The Museum of Fenland Drainage, Ely
- Biggar Gasworks Museum, Scottish Borders
- The virtual Museum of Airsickness Bags which, in October 2006, was exhibiting 1,184 'attractive and unique motion-discomfort receptacles purloined from several hundred different airlines'

In the end the *Diary* hailed the Museum of Lead Mining at Wanlockhead, Scotland, which comprises, reader Frank Naylor reported, 'A large number of lumps of ore in glass cases, the glass cases being considerably more interesting.'

Guardian

Stuart Conway runs a website offering to pop people's messages into a bottle and hurl them into the sea off Brighton.

Over ten years he has launched 6,000 bottled messages free of charge. He knows of just 20 which have been found – in Brittany, the Netherlands and Germany.

Daily Mail

When London Zoo erected a sign saying 'Annual Stock Take. Please Queue Here', *The Times* published a picture of the sign with a line of Jackass penguins obediently forming a queue.

Chapter 21

SERVICE LIFE

A 22-year-old soldier, recently returned from Iraq, put a firework between his buttocks during a display in Sunderland. A friend lit the blue touch paper and retired. The soldier was admitted to hospital for treatment on a scorched colon.

The Times reported: 'Experts said that launching a rocket from the backside contravened the firework code.'

The former member of the Household Cavalry said later: 'I constantly feel as if I have eaten the hottest curry in the world. I can safely say I won't be doing it again.'

Sunday Times/Sunday Mail

Todd Dunn, of Ferndown, Dorset, recalled that during his time in the Senior Service There were three categories of bad behaviour due to drink:

- Junior ratings were drunk.
- Senior ratings were confused.
- Officers were high-spirited.

Daily Telegraph

Health and Safety officials have decreed that soldiers learning to play the bagpipes should wear earplugs.

Tests show that bagpipes outdoors can reach 111 decibels, slightly louder than a pneumatic drill. Indoors it's 116 decibels (as loud as a chainsaw).

Daily Telegraph

The *Telegraph*'s leader pointed out the dangers of 'losing a brave and noble tradition. For hundreds of years the skirl of the pipes has inspired our men and struck fear into our enemies.' It pointed out that some pipers have won the Victoria Cross for playing while injured and under fire.

'What these men would say about the cowardice and officiousness of the latest ruling doesn't bear thinking about.'

There was no mention, though, of the old adage which has it that bagpipes are an ill wind that nobody blows good.

Daily Telegraph

D-Day was looming and paratrooper Lieutenant Stan Jeavons was refused leave to see his first-born son. Instead he joined others aboard a military Dakota taking troops to the South Coast. In mid-flight Stan realised he was flying over his West Midlands home so he opened the hatch and jumped out. Hours later, when he arrived home in Coseley, Dudley, two military policemen were waiting for him.

Stan told the MPs they could do it the hard way – and tapped his Sten gun – or they could let him inside to hold his baby and then go quietly.

He got his five minutes and avoided a court martial because D-Day was so close. He then became the first officer to parachute into occupied France.

In January 2007 Stan died aged 88 and his son said: 'Had he been killed I would have known that he had held me and kissed me and told me he loved me. This is one of the greatest treasures of my life.'

Sun

In the 1940s the following Admiralty Fleet Order was issued:

'Their Lordships wish to bring it to the attention of all ratings that exposure to the ship's radar… will in no way affect their manly attributes.' This in a letter from Lord Balfour of Burleigh, Fife – a former Leading Radio Electrician's Mate RN – who goes on to say that 'I and those radar mechanics with whom I kept in touch were all successful in producing children.'

The Times

Stephen Eggar, of Swanage, Dorset, remembers when, in 1947, he was posted to Mons Barracks for officer training under Regimental Sergeant Major Ronnie Brittain:

'What a character: well over 6ft tall and weighing (at a guess) more than 20 stone. He rode a utilitarian but pristine, khaki-painted Army-issue bicycle and we wondered if it had been specially strengthened. He ruled with a rod of iron but was always fair. Even the CO would not step onto his parade ground without getting the RSM's permission... Mrs Brittain was also a disciplinarian. Woe betide any soldier of whatever rank observed by her to be improperly dressed or walking slovenly. She would immediately call "Ronnie" and send him out to apprehend the culprit.'

Daily Mail

Chapter 22

A TOUCH OF CLASS

Sir Thomas Beecham once ran into a lady in Fortnum and Mason. He did not recognise her but vaguely recalled that she had a sister. He asked what her sister was up to these days and the lady replied: 'Oh, you know, still Queen.'

Sunday Times magazine

Judith Oliver of Harrogate writes to *The Times* about an Edwardian speaker at the Royal Horticultural Society who said: 'No matter how small your garden, always leave an acre to grow wild.'

The Times

For many years the Carlton Club has been resisting the idea of women members. In July 2006 *The Times* reported 'widespread spluttering outrage' when it was discovered that the voice used by the new 'talking elevator' was that of – a woman.

The Times

In class-conscious Britain you can be judged by how you knot your tie.

Daily Telegraph reader Jeremy Tozer, of Teignmouth, Devon, opined: 'The Windsor is large, unpleasant, flashy – and named after someone who did not do his duty, and is therefore not suitable for a gentleman.'

Richard Stevens, of Oxford, felt that: 'Windsor knots are intimately associated with Brylcreem and brothel creepers, and are simply non-U.

Daily Telegraph

Asda's stores in the South of England report increased sales of flat caps, and a spokesman said that they were no longer the badge of the 'whippet-loving, pigeon-fancying working-class man drinking a pint of mild. Now you're more likely to hear the typical flat-cap wearer saying "Absolutely marvellous darling", rather than "Trouble at t-mill".'

Daily Telegraph

Simpsons in the Strand don't allow women in trousers in their restaurant. E. Montague, of St Leonard's on Sea, East Sussex, went there wearing a smart velvet trouser suit and was told by the maitre d' that if she cared to take her trousers off he would ensure that she was seated behind a pillar.

Daily Mail

Henry Button of Cambridge writes of a friend who began work at the Home Office in 1936. He took a stroll in St James's without a hat. He was spotted by his superior officer who told him that Home Office gentlemen wore hats in the Park.

Daily Telegraph

It's tough at the top. Andrew Marr writes that he was interviewing 'the glorious Helen Mirren' at Claridges, and was told:

'If you are a starry customer who sashays into London once a year for Wimbledon or whatever, you can leave your clothes and other belongings where they fall. Claridges will photograph the room exactly as you left it and then pack away your stuff. When you return you find your belongings exactly how you left them – and it's as if you'd never left.'

Daily Telegraph

In May 2006 it was reported that England's first holiday camp opened 100 years ago at Caister, near Great Yarmouth, on the chilly Norfolk coast. It was founded by avowed socialist and teetotaller John Fletcher Dodd and was called Dodd's Socialist Holiday Camp.

Dodd set up the camp to provide holidays for the working classes, and it was run as if it were an Army boot camp. The jolly holidaymakers were roused from their beds at 7am. Alcohol, gambling, bad language and talking after 11pm were banned. Anyone caught sneaking out for a pint at the local pub was fined or thrown out.

Prices were relatively high. In 1914, the cost of a week in a tent was one guinea per person – just a little less than the average weekly wage.

Dodd himself was not totally committed to the regime of camp life. He used to take his family on exotic holidays in Switzerland.

Daily Mail

In May 2006 the *Daily Telegraph* carried an article on Sir John Ellerman asking 'Was This the Richest British Tycoon Ever?'

The next day, C. D. Fisher of Chester wrote recalling how Sir John and his wife used to stay occasionally at the Anglesey Arms Hotel in Menai Bridge. They would sit in the hotel lounge and order 'a pot of tea for one please, and two cups'.

Daily Telegraph

George Orwell once wrote that England was the most class-ridden country in the world – 'ruled largely by the old and the silly'.

According to a poll published in August 2006, class still matters in Britain. The most useful markers to identify class are occupation, address, accent and income – according to a poll in the *Economist*.

Wealth alone does not indicate class and it is difficult, if not impossible, to change one's class. Two-thirds of those questioned said they were born into a class and their children will be born into the same class.

Daily Telegraph/Economist

Times reader Andrew May of Wimbledon writes: 'At school we were taught that a letter to a gentleman should be addressed Esq. If writing to a greengrocer you used Mr.'

The Times

A 19-year-old ladette went on a TV course to learn how to be a lady and met and fell in love with a viscount. After the affair broke up she said she had no regrets.

'I do feel posher now. I used to get plastered on vodka, but now I prefer Pernod and blackcurrant.'

And she passed on some tips on becoming a lady: 'Don't flash your boobs in public. Wipe lipstick off a boy's face after a snog. Eat off a plate, not out of the frying pan.'

News of the World

The widow of a devoted Newcastle United fan got him a solid granite tombstone in the shape of a footballer's shirt in the Toon's black and white stripes. The inscription says simply 'DAD 1'.

The Times

Chapter 23

COUNCIL DAZE

The Northumberland parish council chairman who led the campaign for a bypass became the first person to crash on it.

Independent on Sunday

Students from Camberwell College of Art spent months restoring a 1960s caravan and turning it into a mobile gallery. Hundreds of hours of work went into making the caravan a pink and white work of art – but the local council towed the van away and crushed it. Said a Southwark council official: 'We regularly take and destroy caravans. How do we know it's art?'

The Times, under the headline 'Council Can't Tell Its Art From Its Eyesore'

After Denise Moon's partner died in 2005, final demands for his council tax kept on coming. To prove that he was not avoiding payment, Denise, of Stockton-on-Tees, took his ashes to court in July 2006.

The Times

Darren Gray was told to remove a flag of St George with the word England on it from the side of his house or face a possible £1,000 fine. Bedford Council said he did not have a licence to advertise.

Darren asked: 'What am I supposed to be advertising?'

'England', he was told.

Daily Telegraph

The *Guardian's Diary* gave its Local Council Employee of the Week Award to Calderdale traffic coordinator Keith Kerrison.

Mr Kerrison was asked what he planned to do about illegal parking. He replied that, in view of his imminent retirement, he planned to do 'absolutely nothing'.

Guardian, quoting from the *Halifax Evening Courier*

East Devon District council has received a complaint about Sid and Alma collecting money for Sidmouth's lifeboat.

They have been wielding their charity buckets in the town for years, standing out all day, come wind, rain or shine. But in 2006 they were reported for not having a collector's licence. To apply for a licence they would have to be over 16 and fill out a form with their name, address, phone number and date of birth.

Sid and Alma are plastic mannequins.

Daily Mail

Terry Wogan signed off his last *Sunday Telegraph* column of 2006 with some of the oddball stories from his readers.

One woman reported that the local council had erected a bus shelter near her home – a bit strange because she does not live on a bus route. A bus stop sign was erected and the shelter was cleaned regularly every month.

The lady rang the council and asked if there was going to be a new bus route. No, she was told – and a notice was added to the bus stop reading: 'Not Operational.'

Sunday Telegraph

Wardens hid in the bushes to try to catch trespassers on the Isle of Wight. But they were made to wear fluorescent jackets after being mistaken for paedophiles.

Isle of Wight County Press

Miss Sylvia Sutherland, a lady in her forties, was prosecuted for non-payment of council tax because she insisted on paying in cash.

She told magistrates that she had taken cash to the council offices once a month but St Albans District Council accepts payment only by direct debit, standing order or cheque.

Miss Sutherland was issued with a liability order to pay the outstanding £477.29 arrears and a £50 summons fee.

Daily Telegraph

A council apologised to 80-year-old Alice Nelson, of Wigan, for sending a debt collector to obtain her 5p rent arrears. It was the first time she had been in arrears in 45 years.

Daily Telegraph

A £60 parking fine was slapped on a lorry in Lanarkshire as the driver lay dead inside his cab. The ticket was later withdrawn.

The Times

Chris Huskinson, 22, has a strip across his windscreen reading: 'I Hate Traffic Wardens'.

A grinning warden slapped a £30 fine on Chris's Fiesta in Birmingham – and had a photograph taken of himself doing it.

Said Chris: 'This makes me hate wardens even more.'

Sun

Lateral thinker Edward de Bono came up with this solution for cities choked with parked cars: 'Scrap parking meters, traffic wardens and penalties and let drivers park anywhere – but they must leave their lights on.'

Andrew Marr, *Daily Telegraph*.

Harry Sas complained to North Somerset Council about dirty streets. The council delivered to him a litter picker, a sweeping brush and plastic sacks – along with an invitation to clean his own street.

Independent on Sunday

Why is one not surprised by this item in the *Guardian Diary*: the new solar-powered lights designed to illuminate city centre trees in Manchester have failed 'because there isn't enough sun.'

Guardian

When Bath began reconstructing its famous thermal baths, the cost was estimated at £13 million. But when the work was finished in the summer of 2006 it was years behind schedule and had cost £45 million.

'The city has been reunited with its soul,' said a Bath tourism councillor.

'Nonsense', said Ross Clark in the *Sunday Telegraph*. 'The goody-goody health and beauty treatments on offer to the public have absolutely nothing to do with the city's soul. If the local council really wanted to evoke the spirit of Bath... they would offer a quick dip in the waters, with copious amounts of snuff followed by a full day's drinking, gambling and whoring. In its eighteenth-century heyday many of the socialites were not there to be cured... some did not go to the baths at all, but hung around the White Hart Inn, where a gentleman could always count upon meeting, and engaging with, a willing prostitute, watched on more than one occasion by Jane Austen.'

Sunday Telegraph

A lorry from the firm Meyers of Stratford got stuck axle-deep in a street in Belsize Park, North London, after the road collapsed beneath it. Before it could be pulled free by another lorry – a traffic warden slapped a ticket on it.

Daily Mail

Police blocked off Great Peter Street in Central London during a political demonstration. Traffic wardens swooped on cars caught in the blockage and one driver said: 'It wasn't just that they were giving everyone tickets. It was the fact that they were laughing about it.'

Westminster Council promised to investigate.

The Times

Bristol city council threatened to confiscate doormats from outside the homes of council tenants saying that 'they pose a tripping hazard'.

Tenants were angry and Roger Perry, 62, said: 'God knows how I've lived here so many years and never heard of any accidents.'

The council sent letters – more than 2,000 of them - headed 'Health and Safety Issues – Hazardous Mats'.

Guardian/Daily Mail

Senior members of Trafford council in Manchester spent £3,200 on a night in the luxury Castle Green Hotel in Kendal to discuss: 'How to maintain services on a tight budget'.

Guardian

Sutton Council decided to make Britney Spears an honorary citizen because she 'named her son after the town'. Council officials promised her 'a five-star welcome if she comes to visit'. This was followed by the *Guardian Diary* which said: 'Guys, we really hate to disappoint you, but... How can we say this? The thing is, we don't actually think... Oh, forget it.'

Sutton Post/Guardian

Terry Wogan, in his column in the *Sunday Telegraph*, quoted one of the listed hazards in the job specification of a Community Safety Officer for Hampshire County Council: 'Exposure to non-ionising radiation.'

'That'll be sunshine, then,' quoth Terry.

Sunday Telegraph

A Colchester, Essex, couple were fined £30 for parking in their own drive because a traffic warden claimed their vehicle's rear end was hanging over double yellow lines.

A photograph in the *Colchester Evening Gazette* showed the car parked in the drive without the boot extending over the yellow lines.

Colchester Evening Gazette

Houses in North Benwell, Newcastle upon Tyne, were sold by the city council for 50p in a desperate attempt to regenerate an area plagued by high unemployment and anti-social behaviour.

Seven years later, in 2007, they were being sold for up to £145,000 each.

Observer

When eighty-mile-an-hour gales lashed Britain in January 2007, Nicky Clegg's car was crushed by a falling tree.

Police told Nicky, 42, of Stoulton, Worcestershire, to leave her Ford Fiesta until she could arrange for it to be towed away. But when she returned to her car next day she had got a parking ticket.

The Times/Daily Mail

What Arthur Bulmer wanted to do with the sand that blew into his garden from the foreshore at St Anne's, Lancashire, was to put it back on the beach. But his local council said that that would constitute fly-tipping on sand which was part of the Queen's Crown Estate.

Under the law Mr Bulmer could face fines of up to £50,000. Continued breaches could land him in jail and see his vehicle – in his case, a wheelbarrow – confiscated.

Daily Telegraph

Residents of a street in Burnley, Lancashire, complained to the council that they suffered from having Neighbours from Hell. They complained of graffiti and yobs milling around in big gangs drinking cider and fighting.

When they learned that the rowdy neighbours were to be evicted, they were jubilant. But joy turned to rage when social services moved the rowdy lot into a house 100 yards away in the same street.

Daily Mirror

Shocked residents of Colmer's Hill, near Bridport, Dorset, complained to their council after reading notices saying that all local trees were to be felled and replaced by telephone masts.

Council officer John Greenslade, whose faked signature appeared on the notices said: 'We get this sort of thing around April 1.'

Daily Telegraph

Chapter 24

LET US PRAY

Dame Sybil Thorndike tells of the day when a naïve clergyman introduced her to a crowded room as 'one of the most famous members of the oldest profession in the world'.

The Times

A book on children's letters to God includes:
- On Halloween I am going to wear a devil's costume. Is that all right with you?
- How come you did all those miracles in the old days and don't do any now?
- Did you mean for giraffes to look like that or was it an accident?

- Thank you for the baby brother, but what I prayed for was a puppy.

Extracts from *Children's Letters to God* compiled by Stuart Hample & Eric Marshall, published by Kyle Cathie, *Daily Mail*

When Mother Teresa met newspaper tycoon Robert Maxwell in 1988 she said she had a message for him from God.

Maxwell's beam didn't last long after she told him that the message was: 'Give £1 million to Mother Teresa'.

Daily Mail

In March 2007 Pope Benedict XVI decided it was time to remind everybody that Hell 'really exists and is eternal – even if nobody talks about it anymore'.

The Times commented: 'It is true that Hell seems to have fallen out of fashion; especially as a place to be feared. Mark Twain praised Heaven for its climate, but firmly recommended Hell "…for the company".'

The Times

Michael Lewis of Hull remembers 'some innocent young theologians' who set up the Cambridge University New Testament Society.

'It was a refreshingly long time before anyone enlightened them,' he writes.

Guardian

A caring Government has promised to be tough on crime – and Lincolnshire police are asking churchgoers to concentrate their prayers on crimes such as burglaries and violent attacks.

The Times

Monks and nuns in closed orders have been told they do not qualify for charitable status – because their prayers do not benefit society.

Daily Mail

The number of worshippers attending services at St Bartholomew's Church in Warleggan, Cornwall, fell dramatically when eccentric Reverend Frederick Densham became vicar in 1931.

He painted the church and the rectory in glaring colours. He put a barbed-wire fence around the rectory gardens and threatened to sell the organ. And the oddball incumbent solved his empty pews problem – by filling them with cardboard cut-outs.

Western Morning News

A tramp walked into a harvest festival service in St Faith's Church, Havant, Hampshire, and started munching his way through fruit, vegetables, raw eggs and a tin of cat food.

The congregation's reaction was typically English – they carried on singing and the clergyman conducting

the service said: 'We thought he had come in to say his prayers.'

Daily Telegraph

Churchgoers in Britain are still highly super-stitious. Centuries of preaching have failed to banish belief in omens and portents of good and bad luck. According to a survey nearly all worshippers admit to practising superstitious behaviour. Research carried out at the University of Wales showed that:

- Eight out of ten admitted to crossing their fingers for luck.
- Just as many had touched wood for protection.
- Seven in ten had thrown spilt salt over their left shoulder.
- About one quarter believed that it was lucky to find a four-leaf clover, to have a black cat cross their path and to see a money spider.
- A similar proportion believed that it was unlucky to open an umbrella indoors and a sixth believed it was unlucky to pass someone on the stairs or walk under a ladder.

Submitted by Ruth Gledhill,
The Times

Chris Moncrieff is a legendary Fleet Street journalist who spent more than 50 years in newspaper journalism – many of them in the cut and thrust of reporting Westminster for the Press Association. But he didn't start attracting hate mail until he retired and took over his local church magazine.

Poisonous missives poured through his letterbox screaming: 'We don't want your Fleet Street ways here.'

'I have never discovered,' writes Chris, 'why I stood accused of producing a red-top style magazine, although I have my suspicions. I have a tendency to fill up empty spaces with quotations':

- 'If all the people who go to sleep in church were laid end to end, they would be a lot more comfortable.' Mrs Robert A Taft
- 'There does not seem very much left for us agnostics not to believe in.' Jed Larsen
- 'I get into bed, turn out the lights, and say b******s to the lot of 'em and go to sleep.' Winston Churchill.

Daily Telegraph

A church weekly notice sheet said: '12 noon. Please join us for lunch. This will be followed by prayers for the sick.'

Spotted by Mrs Pauline Sunderland,
Ringwood, Hampshire, *Daily Mail*

Villagers in Rainbow, near Macclesfield, Cheshire, knew there was something odd about the peal of bells coming from their parish church. They went to check – and found the vicar had locked himself in and was ringing out the SOS signal.

Daily Express/Daily Telegraph

'God created Man and granted him dominion over every creeping thing that creepeth upon the Earth,' according to the Book of Genesis. Thus wrote *Times* Religion Correspondent Ruth Gledhill, and she went on:

'But when it came to one of the creepiest things of all, bats, God made an exception of His own special representatives on Earth. The Bishop of Ripon and Leeds, the Right Rev. John Packer, had to defer his moving plans for at least a year while architects struggled to accommodate two species of protected bats found in a coach house bought for him by the Church Commissioners.

'Britain's strict conservation laws called for the bats to have a bat run built for them in the roof of the coach house and a heated bat box in the boiler room.

'A spokesman for the Bishop said: "Bishop John is happy to be sharing his new home with these rare creatures. As long as they are happy, so is he."'

The Times

Chapter 25

MIND YOUR LANGUAGE

Corinne and Dai Male, of Ibstock, Leicestershire, tell of the north-west Leicestershire man who took his cat to the vet.

'Is it a tom?' asked the vet.

'Nay, maister, I've brought him with me.'

Guardian

The classic definition of chutzpah is: 'Man murders both parents and pleads for clemency because he is an orphan.'

Daily Telegraph letter

Hull City Council's Corporate Equalities Unit has sent out emails saying that the following words are now unacceptable: ladies, girls, pet, duck, luvvie, flower, lasses, love, darling, and sweetheart.

The correct word to cover all of these terms is 'women'. Critics point out that the banned words are traditional terms of endearment and Liberal Democrat councillor Carl Minns said: 'It's political correctness gone mad.'

Daily Mail

Computers trained to filter 'unsuitable' words and phrases were discussed in the *Guardian*'s Diary.

While Scunthorpe understandably becomes S****horpe and Blackpool becomes Black***l it seems that 'entitled', 'parse' and 'Saturday' survive intact.

Guardian readers were quick to add place names to which the computer filter might object: Prickwillow in Cambridgeshire and Cockermouth in Cumbria. Diarist Jon Henley signed off with 'our personal favourite' – Mount Mee in Queensland.

Guardian

The phrase 'Brass monkey weather' goes back to the Napoleonic wars when a ship's cannonballs were stored in brass racks known as monkeys. In cold weather the balls shrank and fell off.

From Robert Allen's *Dictionary of English Phrases*, *Daily Express*

A London tour guide is quoted as having said to a group of Americans: 'Over there is the London School of Economics where the students include your very own Monica Lewinsky. I believe she has recently done well in her orals.'

The guide paused and then added: 'That's what we call spoken exams.'

The Times

Film subtitles are often distorted by bad translations because they are outsourced to the Far East where subtitlers are cheaper. Mauled subtitles have included:

- **'Flying into an asteroid field' became 'Flying into a steroid field'.**
- **'She died in a freak rugby accident' became 'She died in a rugby match for people with deformities'.**
- **'You've got ivory skin' became 'You've got skin like an elephant'.**
- **'Killed by meningitis' became 'Killed by men in nighties'.**

Sun/The Times

Shakespeare spelt his name in several ways, including Shaksper – but never as Shakespeare.

The longest word he used is 'honorificabilitudinitas' in Love's Labour's Lost. It is an extension of 'honorificabilis' meaning 'honorableness'.

Daily Express

Of the 24,000 words used by Shakespeare some 1,700 were his own inventions: besmirch, anchovy, shudder and impede among them.

The Times

In his book *Beyond Words*, Radio 4 presenter John Humphrys complains about the way Shakespeare is converted into young-person speak.

He cites a horrible example from Macbeth: 'Is this a dagger I see before me' becomes 'Oooh! Would you look at that.'

Simon Hoggart, *Guardian*

Newcastle council issued a directive to staff recommending them to refrain from calling people 'hinny', 'pet', 'love', 'darling' or 'sweetheart'.

There were howls of protest at this and the *Independent*'s John Walsh told how he was always charmed by barmaids who greeted him with ''allo 'andsome, what you 'avin?'

Independent

This was followed by a charming letter in *The Times* from Her Royal Highness Princess Helen of Romania, who gave her address as Haswell, Co. Durham:

'I am often called Princess Pet in local shops and feel that I am accepted and included as part of the community.'

The Times

A book on UK dialects, slang and regional accents throws up:

- Brassic: broke, lacking money – London and the South East (boracic lint – skint)
- 'ansome: excellent– Cornwall
- Up the stick: pregnant – Midlands
- Mardle: to gossip – East Anglia
- Mither: to fuss – Lancashire
- Happen: perhaps – Yorkshire
- Docker's doorstep: big crusty piece of bread – Liverpool
- Divvent: don't – Northumbria
- Blootered: drunk – Scotland

Excerpts from Talking for Britain by Simon Elmes,
Daily Express

The Queen's English is growing more like ours, innit? A scientific study of the Queen's Christmas broadcasts claims that she 'is drifting slowly towards speaking Estuary English. Her speech has followed a general trend from cut-glass URP (Upper Received Pronunciation) towards a more democratic Standard Received Pronunciation and its close relative Standard Southern British English. The study suggests the royal vowel sounds have undergone a subtle evolution since the days when coal was delivered to Buckingham Palace in 'sex'.

- In 1952 the Monarch announced: 'I em

speaking to you from my own hame, where
I am spending Christmas with my femly.'
- In 1962: 'A merry Christmas and a happay
New Yeah.'
- In 2005: 'I hope you will have a very
happee Christmas and thet you go into
the New Year with renewed hope and
confidence.'
    Daily Telegraph and *Independent on Sunday*,
        under the headline 'My 'Ubby and I, Innit.'

**A letter from a holiday company said: 'We apologise for
any incontinence caused by this uncontrollable
situation.'**

Spotted by Diana Spires, Alcester, Warwickshire,
Daily Mail

Philip Norman is collecting malapropisms and
plans to turn them into a book. Some gems from
his collection:
- The couple who decided not to marry
because they'd been happily co-rabbiting
for years
- The woman who urged her boyfriend to
wear a condominium
- The swimmer who told of a jellyfish
wrapping its testicles around her
- A visitor to Bali enjoyed sunsets containing
all the colours of the rectum

- The dog-lover with a sausage-shaped Datsun
- The schoolboy learning about St Paul's conversion on the road to Domestos
- Salome did the Dance of the Seven Veils in front of Harrods
- Having only one wife is called monotony

Daily Mail (which will be pleased to pass on any malaprops you know)

A.D.C. Lund, of Great Missenden, Buckinghamshire, wondered if a gathering of headmasters should be called a peck of beaks.

Daily Telegraph

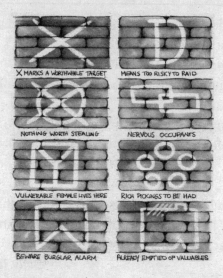

X MARKS A WORTHWHILE TARGET

MEANS TOO RISKY TO RAID

NOTHING WORTH STEALING

NERVOUS OCCUPANTS

VULNERABLE FEMALE LIVES HERE

RICH PICKINGS TO BE HAD

BEWARE BURGLAR ALARM

ALREADY EMPTIED OF VALUABLES

These are not childish drawings illustrating some playground game – they are the kind of symbols sometimes used to tell villains if your house is worth burgling. Reading from top to bottom they mean:

- X marks a worthwhile target
- D means too risky to raid
- O with a X over it means nothing worth stealing
- Two interlocking rectangles warns of nervous occupants
- Y inside a square says a vulnerable female lives here
- Three circles means rich pickings to be had
- A symbol looking like an upside down paper hat warns: Beware – burglar alarm
- A house with three slashes through its roof says: Already emptied of valuables

The eight symbols are thought to be specific to the area around Walsall in the West Midlands and an expert in criminal psychology said, 'Some markings mean something else in other towns and cities.'

Daily Mail

Chapter 26

GOLDEN OLDIES

When 60-year-old Helen Mirren won a best actress award her local paper carried the headline: 'Wapping Pensioner Wins Hollywood Oscar'.

Guardian/East London Advertiser

When Edwina MacKenzie reached 90 she credited her long life to having decided to get off the Titanic after it hit an iceberg.

Globe & Mail, Toronto

Jane Kiehl tells of the days when she organised activities for the residents of an old people's home. A popular game was completing well-known phrases. For example, the two words 'better safe' required the response 'than sorry'. On one occasion the words on offer were 'make love' with the expected response being 'not war'.

Jane writes: 'I had barely got the first two words out when a 90-year-old shouted "While you can."'

Reader's Digest

Edith Wright, 93, won the Zimmer Frame race at her rest home in Christchurch, Dorset.

Sun

Great grandfather Geoffrey Scalbert, a retired teacher from Shaftesbury, Dorset, celebrated his hundredth birthday in July 2006.

He has smoked since he was 11 and gets through 30 a day. He drinks a large whisky every night and has lived with five women. 'That's my secret for a long and happy life,' he says.

The Times

Jack Archer was asked to prove that he was over 18 when he wanted to buy a bottle of sherry in a York supermarket. Jack fought in France in World War II, is a former Lord Mayor of York and was awarded the MBE.

Said Jack: 'I like to think of myself as a youthful 87-year-old, but it would be a stretch to pass myself off as a teenager.'

Daily Mail

Irene, 68, and Ron Jones, 75, are a superstitious couple. They never walk under ladders. Avoid crossing on the stairs. Throw salt over their left shoulder. And suffer from a touch of paraskevidekatriaphobia (the psychological term for the morbid and irrational fear of Friday the thirteenth). So Friday the thirteenth 2006 was a day when Irene might consider not bothering to buy a Lottery ticket – especially after breaking a mirror in their home in Bilston, West Midlands.

But she forgot about the date – and scooped £9.3million.

Daily Express/Daily Mail

A group of pensioners were in their deckchairs enjoying the Redland Wind Band playing in Grove Park, Weston-super-Mare. Some drunken yobs turned up with crates of lager and a football. The yobs yelled abuse at the bandsmen and kicked their ball into the grandstand.

Redland struck up the theme from *The Great Escape* and, as one, a Dad's Army of some 20 veterans, some with sticks, rose from their deckchairs and advanced, shoulder to shoulder. The yobs fled. The veterans returned to their deckchairs amid cheers.

Les Brown, 78, a former World War II RAF pilot, said: 'We got fed up with these little toerags. The *Great Escape* music came on and I looked round and there were others obviously thinking the same .

as me. We stood up and kissed our wives and marched towards them. Those youngsters didn't stand a chance in hell. I've never seen a group of young men look so scared as we started advancing.'

One ageing warrior said: 'Maybe it was the Dunkirk spirit that spurred us on.'

The Times, *Guardian* and *Sun* with a picture of the pensioners captioned: 'Who do you think you kidding, little Hitlers?'

Ada Mason, Britain's oldest woman, of Upton, near Leeds, died aged 111 in February 2007. She was six when Queen Victoria died. She ascribed her longevity to a daily helping of bread and dripping sprinkled with salt.

She leaves 12 grandchildren, 'at least' 20 great-grandchildren and a total of great-great-grandchildren which relatives have yet to work out.

Guardian

Vera Howarth celebrated her ninety-eighth birthday in June 2006 – with a cake older than she was.

A seven-tier fruit cake was made in 1895 (when Queen Victoria was on the throne) for the wedding of Vera's parents. Most of it was eaten, but the top tier was lovingly kept by the family.

'It still smells beautiful,' she said.

Daily Telegraph

Constance Brown was 98 when she got an MBE in 2006.

She and her husband Sidney opened their fish and chip shop in Main Street, Pembroke, in 1928, and she is still dispensing fish and chips from the same shop.

She says her long life is down to a daily dish of fish-and-chips and no veg.

Independent/Independent on Sunday

Les Lailey celebrated his golden wedding by eating tinned chicken that was 50 years old. The Buxted Whole Cooked Chicken in Jelly was part of a hamper Les and his wife Beryl, both 73, received on their wedding day. 'It went down a treat,' said Les. 'Now I am going to save the empty tin as a keepsake.'

Sun

Tony Newell of Exmouth, Devon, sent in a Q&A to the *Daily Mail* about the delights of retirement:

Q - When is a retiree's bedtime?

A – Three hours after he falls asleep on the couch.

Q – How many retirees does it take to change a light bulb?

A – Only one – but it might take all day.

Q – What do retirees call a long lunch?

A – Normal.

Q – What's the biggest advantage of going back to school as a retiree?
A – If you skip lessons no one calls your parents.

Daily Mail

On 26 July 2006 the *Daily Mail* reported that every day for the past seventy-seven years George Millar, 93, of Clydebank, has shaved with the same razor – a Gillette which cost him one shilling (seven and a half pence). He even has the original copper box which came with the razor and he says that 'now and then' his 1929 razor needs a new blade.

Daily Mail

In September 2006 'Buster' Martin's firm, as a special concession, gave him a day off _ to celebrate his hundredth birthday. Buster's birthday plans had been to work as usual and celebrate afterwards by having a pint on his way home from Pimlico Plumbers in South London.

Mr Martin, a widower with 17 children and 70 grandchildren, admits he lost count of his great-grandchildren 'years ago'. He has never owned a telephone because 'they are a bloody nuisance. You can be sitting peacefully indoors and they start ringing. I hate them.'

Britain's oldest worker tried retirement but did not like it. He said: 'If I did not work I would become a miserable sod.'

Daily Telegraph

Gwen Dorling got into the spirit of things when a surprise male stripper turned up at her birthday party. She cavorted with him at her home in Diss, Norfolk, and said: 'He was a bit of all right.'

Gwen was celebrating reaching the age of 102.

Daily Telegraph

At a time when newspapers were full of angry stories about Gordon Brown stealthily squirrelling away zillions of pounds worth of pension funds there was a smidgeon of cheer from the Department for Work and Pensions which announced increases in state pensions and benefits from 9 April 2007.

Among other changes it revealed the joyous news that: 'If you are 80 or over you will be entitled to £0.25 a week Age Addition.'

Pension Service pamphlet BR2 189 02/07

A sign by a river in Selby, Yorkshire, reads: 'RIVER RESCUE. In the event of falling into river, dial 999, ask for Police/Fire, indicating you need river rescue.'

Spotted by Hilary Gigg of Hambleton,
North Yorkshire, *Daily Mail*

Chapter 27

JUST THE JOB

Michael Leamons tells how he was not attracted to a job as a sewage plant attendant after spotting that one of the requirements was 'Must be able to swim'.

Reader's Digest

Some firms have banned their employees from sending birthday cards joking about their colleagues advancing years.

The *Daily Mail* said: 'To hell with political correctness' – and printed a page full of ageist jokes, such as:

Q: What is the best birth control method for OAPs?

A: Nudity.

Daily Mail

Debra Donath reports a notice received at work: 'Due to building work your office may be either cooler or warmer than usual on Tuesday. Dress accordingly.'

Submitted by A. Graber, *Reader's Digest*

Cliff Woodcraft, of Sheffield, puts forward the view that daytime TV is a government scheme to discourage workers from taking days off sick.

Independent

The CareerBuilder.com website reports on excuses offered by staff arriving late for work:

- **I went all the way to the office in my pyjamas and had to go back home to change.**
- **I couldn't find the right tie, so I waited for the shops to open**
- **I dreamed that I had been fired, so didn't bother to get out of bed.**

Independent on Sunday

An organisation with 3,500 employees recorded more than 500 accidents in a three and a half year period. There were 154 slips, trips or falls. A wet tea room floor was responsible for one worker suffering a groin strain. Others slipped on a raisin, tripped over a bin, slipped on a plastic bag, walked into a warning sign, got a burn from a toaster, got scalded by a boiler and one bruised an eye when a lavatory roll dispenser fell from a wall.

All this at the Health and Safety Executive. The HSE conceded that the incident rate was high but said that it strived to set high standards in the reporting of mishaps.

In *The Times* the story was headlined: 'It's a Dangerous Life Working at the HQ of Health and Safety'.

The Times

Car salesman Steve Moseley, of Gosport, Hampshire, scratched away to reveal the numbers on his £1 million Lotto card and then danced on his desk, threw all the money in his wallet at colleagues, sent out for champagne and quit his job.

But when he rang the National Lottery to claim his million they told him that he had misread the numbers.

Sun

In April 2006 there were reports of scientists developing a more efficient alternative to the electric light bulb. This inspired the *Daily Mail* to run a feature headlined: 'At Least It Will Mean an End to Jokes Like These':

Q: *How many folk singers does it take to change a light bulb?*

A: Five. One to change it and four to sing about how good the old one was.

Q: How many voyeurs does it take to change a light bulb?

A: Only one, but they'd much rather watch someone else do it.

Q: How many workmen does it take to change a light bulb?

A: Three. One to turn up when you are out. One to change the switch and one to bring along the wrong kind of bulb.

Daily Mail

Undercover investigators for Surrey County Council found that a roadworks gang did less than one hour of genuine work in an eight-hour shift.

While the team was supposed to be working they had been shopping, chatting, driving around, drinking tea and reading.

Evening Standard/Daily Telegraph

In May 2006 Paul Anderson, 47, was hailed as Britain's longest-serving TV extra. For some twenty years he has had a non-speaking role in almost every episode of the BBC's hospital drama *Casualty* – usually pushing a trolley. The highlight of his TV career came in 1966 when the character he plays won £500 in a lottery. He was allowed to break his silence to say how pleased he was.

Sunday Times

More than 100 senior civil servants on leadership courses studied Shakespeare plays in an attempt to improve their decision making and leadership skills. Among the Bard's plays deemed to be most relevant to the workings of modern Government were:

- Henry V – 'to help participants to live their leadership potential to the full'
- Julius Caesar – 'all about surviving power struggles at the very top'
- Macbeth – 'offering valuable lessons about courageous leadership and ethical ambition'

The report is headlined: 'Friends, Romans, Bureaucrats', with the opening sentence being: 'Once more unto the brief dear friends, once more.'

Sunday Telegraph

It was hot in the kitchens of an Italian restaurant in Carlisle. Then some of the staff began developing impressive tans – and later blisters and headaches. Health and Safety officials investigated and discovered that sunbed bulbs had mistakenly been fitted to the lights intended to kill flies.

Daily Telegraph

A postwoman was taken off her round covering the North Yorkshire village of Kellington because her employers thought she spent too much time chatting to friendly villagers.

She was transferred to a more urban route in Goole.

The Times

There was a report that workers were often confused by bosses' business jargon – in particular the phrase 'blue sky thinking'.

The *Guardian* came to the rescue with: 'It is intended to encourage people to think huge, limitless thoughts. In reality it gives people an excuse to stare out of the window.'

Guardian

An expert has revealed some of the tricks estate agents use to get people to view unpopular properties:

- 'A bijou home with potential' means tiny and needing a lot of work.
- A photograph taken from the rear of the property means the road at the front is too busy for the estate agent to stand in and take a photograph.
- Descriptions that go on and on about the property being in a good school catchment area could mean the house is not worth mentioning.
- 'Will allow discerning buyer to refurbish to own tastes' means the property has not been looked after or has been badly done.

- 'A compact garden' means not big enough to swing a cat in.

  Daily Telegraph

However, South London estate agent Roy Brooks became famous for being refreshingly honest.

- He once described a house in Wimbledon as 'not fearfully attractive'.
- A six-room house in Chelsea was advertised as: 'Whilst not wishing to gloss over its slum-like qualities, we ought to mention that our clients will sell only to a person with the taste and means to restore it properly.'
- The ad went on to add that 'there is a foul little garden at the back'.

  Daily Telegraph

Video recruitment website www.jobs2view.com has compiled a list of stupid job titles with the winner being: Vision Clearance Executive (window cleaner), closely followed by:

- Education Centre Nourishment Production Assistant (dinner lady)
- Waste Removal Engineer (binman)
- Domestic engineer (housewife)
- Knowledge Navigator (teacher)

  Daily Telegraph

The Santa Claus stationed in Paisley shopping centre's grotto near Glasgow was forced to swap his red hat for a hard hat after being bombarded with mince pies by youths.

Guardian

Chapter 28

CHRISTMAS PRESENCE

Mrs Janice Stone, of Hull, tells of children singing carols at the local old folks' home. A friend's four-year-old grandson was asked if the oldsters had enjoyed the carols.

'Yes,' he replied, 'except for the dead one at the front.'

Daily Mail

The five-year-old grandson of Mrs Lesley Mills of Wolverhampton was one of the three kings in his school's nativity play. She asked him what he had given to Jesus – gold, frankincense or myrrh. The boy said he didn't know, but the box looked like a McDonald's Happy Meal.

Daily Mail

Instead of baubles, Tate Britain's Christmas tree featured models of cherubs complete with explicit depictions of their private parts.

Daily Mail

The *Sunday Times* had some fun with a whole page headlined 'Merry Christmas... from Elf and Safety'. Among the hilarious pieces of advice were these two:

- If you have a fairy at the top of your tree you should be aware that the word 'fairy' can cause offence. A more appropriate term would be 'wand bearer'.
- Do not stand under mistletoe as it can lead to unexpected pregnancy.

Sunday Times

The 2006 Christmas card from the Commission for Racial Equality features a nativity scene and is presented as a draft upon which politically correct comments have been scribbled, such as:

- The snow looks hideously white.
- The animals pulling the sleigh should be products of equal opportunities employment policies, not all one species.
- Stable not compliant with housing code – where is disabled access?
- Sheep should look more diverse.
- Three Wise Men can't be all men.

Daily Mail

It's the ultimate Christmas gift for men – a new Giant
Swiss Army knife which has 85 devices, weighs 2lb
and costs nearly £500. Its devices include:

- A golf club face cleaner.
- Fish hook disgorger
- Cigar cutter
- Flashlight
- Magnifying glass with screwdriver
- Can opener
- Adjustable pliers
- Flat-nose pliers
- Needle-nosed pliers with wire cutter
- Phillips screwdriver
- Metal file
- Round needle file
- Compass
- Ruler
- Scissors
- Allen wrench
- Allen key
- Bottle-top lifter
- Tyre gauge
- 2½in knife blade

It does not, however, have a device for getting
stones out of horses' hooves. This is, apparently,
a myth.

When Chris Bonnington headed a Himalayan
expedition in 1970 he used every blade in his Swiss
Army knife except the fish scaler. He apologised for

this, explaining that there are no fish on the south face of Annapurna.

Guardian

The *Sunday Telegraph* called this 'the shaggiest, most unbelievable Christmas story of all':

At Santa's Magical Animal Kingdom in Westmeath, Ireland, staff were looking forward to their Christmas feast – but someone forgot to secure the pen of their Bactrian camel Gus. This immense, shaggy, intimidating Ship of the Desert escaped and headed for the festive table. Gus is described as 'about the size of a small elephant with large yellow, prominent front teeth'. By the time staff turned up for their party Gus had scoffed more than 200 mince pies and all the crisps and sandwiches and was on his sixth can of Guinness.

Trapeze artist Amanda Sandow said: 'The mess was appalling. It was like a bomb had gone off. He'd eaten the lot. We were pretty angry at the time, but we soon forgave him. He's a lovable rogue and who can blame him for celebrating Christmas.'

How does a camel open a can of Guinness? 'With no bother at all', said 14-year-old Clodagh Cleary. 'He was biting the tops off with his big strong teeth and sucking up the Guinness. It was brilliant.'

Kate Kiernan said: 'Sandwiches for 20 people and 200 mince pies would be nothing for him. It must all go in his humps, we reckon.'

Sunday Telegraph

Scrooge is alive, if not very well. He was out and about grizzling 'Bah! Humbug!' across the nation in the run-up to the 2006 festive season:

- A survey of 23,000 employers revealed that 74 per cent banned Xmas decoration because of fears that followers of other faiths might be upset.

Sun

- Actors at a Preston pantomime were banned from throwing sweets to children in the audience.

Daily Mail

- A Santa was prevented from touring Leighton Buzzard, Bedfordshire, because his sleigh did not have a seatbelt. The town's Round Table have been towing Santa around in a float for 45 years.

Sun

- For the first time in 250 years, children will not be allowed to carry candles at Chelmsford Cathedral's Christingle service in case their hair catches fire. There is no record of this happening since the services began in 1747.

Daily Telegraph

- Villagers in Embsay, North Yorkshire, were told that their festive party would be cancelled unless they carried out a 'risk assessment' on mince pies made by the Women's Institute.

  Sun

- For 40 years the Torbay Gospelaires sang carols in the wards of their local hospital. In 2006 they were banned from the wards for fear of infection.

  Daily Telegraph

Trust the Irish to cock a snoot at Scrooges. Children there often put out sacks instead of socks for Santa to fill. It is traditional to leave out mince pies and a bottle of Guinness for the old fellow.

The Times

The Bishop of Southwark denied being drunk during an incident in which he lost his belongings and suffered head injuries after a 2006 Christmas party at the Irish Embassy in London.

Times Online

Earlier a *Times* leader told its readers that the annual party at the Irish Embassy had a reputation for hospitality so generous that 'guests have been known to cling to the pavement all the way home for fear of falling off'.

The Times

Stuart Prebble, creator of TV's *Grumpy Old Men* series, has a grumpy old look at Christmas and says of pantomimes that in the good old days they were aimed at kids and were full of silly jokes and slapstick.

'Now they're all sex, smut and double entendres. Even the phrase 'He's behind you' carries a whole different meaning.'

From a selection of Prebble's seasonal bleatings in his book *Grumpy Old Christmas*, Weidenfeld & Nicholson, *Daily Mail*

Have a merry festive season and don't read this. The Royal Society for the Prevention of Accidents reports that more than 6,000 people will end up in hospital on Christmas day and that during the 12 days of Christmas more than 80,000 will visit A&E wards. There will be:

- Drunken dads who have severed fingers while trying to carve the turkey
- Chefs who have not followed the correct lifting procedure when moving 24lb turkeys
- More than 1,000 injuries caused by Christmas trees (branches in eyes or people falling off chairs reaching to put the fairy on top)
- Fires caused by lighting candles on Christmas trees and positioning candles underneath strings of cards
- Heavy gifts hidden on top of wardrobes falling off and causing head injuries

- Screwdrivers driven through the palm while trying to penetrate packaging
- Knives slashing through flesh while cutting through thick layers of sticky tape.

Guardian G2

The Santa Claus working in Paisley's shopping centre near Glasgow was forced to swap his red hat for a hard hat after being bombarded with mince pies by youths.

Guardian

In the run-up to the festive season newspapers and magazines vie with each other to provide alleged hangover cures, old and new.

The *Daily Telegraph* magazine filled a page under the headline: 'Are There Hangover Cures That Actually Work?' It listed five 'hangover helpers' ranging in price from £4.99 (RU 21 tablets) to £15.39 (Planetary Herbal Kudzu Complex capsules), and ended up with a last paragraph quoting an expert whose research concluded that 'there was not a lot of evidence for cures... In the end, nothing can prevent or treat hangovers – the only thing is not to drink.'

Daily Telegraph magazine (Sorry. Merry Christmas and a Happy New Year anyway.)

A *Daily Telegraph* reader remembered receiving a Christmas gift from the Mayor of Stalybridge during World War II. It contained a jar of Brylcreem and a packet of razor blades.

'I was in the Women's Auxiliary Service,' writes Joan Brown of Bowness-on-Windermere, Cumbria.

Daily Telegraph

Simon Hoggart's Saturday column in the *Guardian* has been delving into Christmas catalogues and finding such essentials as:

- An easy-clean fibreglass Petstep (£67.50) – a gangplank to allow dogs to stroll into the car boot without having to be lifted onto the protective blanket (£72.95).
- Battery-powered insole heaters.
- A Self-Stirring Mug (£10.95).
- But Simon hadn't realised how long Christmas catalogues have been around until Robin Dow wrote from Sheffield about a Victorian version which offered a walking cane that converted into a small stepladder in case the owner met a mad dog.

Guardian

Prince Charles

'Did I get the ears right, Sir?' was the headline the *Daily Mail* used alongside a sketch of the Prince of Wales by eight-year-old Hugo Marsh, of Davenies School in Beaconsfield, Buckinghamshire. It showed the prince with almost Dumbo-sized ears.

The *Mail*'s assessment of Hugo's artistic efforts was: 'The nose was wonky and the hair a little on the sparse side, but the ears were perfect.'

Prince Charles giggled when he saw the red crayon sketch and Hugo said later, 'I think it looks like him.'

Daily Mail

Chapter 29

ODDS AND SODS

In August 2006 there was a vote for the funniest one-liner in TV comedy history. The winner was Peter Kay for the line from his *Phoenix Nights*: 'Garlic bread – it's the future. I've tasted it.'

Many critics challenged this and suggested ones which they thought were better. David Lister in the Independent recalled one of his favourites – Tony Hancock, making this impassioned plea to fellow jurors:

'Does Magna Carta mean nothing to you? Did she die in vain?'

Independent

BBC2's Newsnight programme interviewed a Welshman who was wearing a T-shirt bearing the message: 'Twll tyn I bob Sais' which, loosely translated, means 'A***holes to the English'.

Daily Telegraph

After a story saying that researchers had calculated that women speak 22,000 words a day, Tony Batcheler, of Kingswood, Surrey, wrote: 'They must have studied remarkably taciturn women.'

The Times

A radio programme asked listeners to name the cruellest lies they had ever heard. One remembered his parents telling him that when ice cream vans switched on their music it meant that they had sold out.

Submitted by Richard Greening, *The Times*

Catherine Miller of Blandford, Dorset, writes of her experience of estate agents' hyperbole. One of them described a property as having a 'view over private water'.

She discovered that the water was the garden pond next door.

Sunday Times

A Cornwall-based company has sold £4 million worth of land on the moon. Moon Estates employ a staff of ten and also offer 'desirable land' on Mars and Venus.

Guardian

Jade Goody went into TV's *Big Brother* house in 2002 and became famous for her 'charming ignorance'.

The show revealed that she thought a ferret was a bird, that Pistachio painted the Mona Lisa, that there was a part of England called East Angular, that Parada was a fashion designer, that there is a language called Portuganese, and that an abscess is a green French drink.

She went on to make a fortune and says: 'I know I am famous for nothing' and insists 'I am not pretending to be thick.'

Guardian

Mike Pitman, of St Helier, Jersey, wanted a CD of the *Last Night of the Proms* and was asked who had written it.

The Times

Alan Porter, of Camberley, Surrey, asked a young assistant in a well-known store for a CD of Mozart's Requiem Mass and was asked: 'Is it a single?'

The Times

Kenneth Williams, of Amersham, Buckinghamshire, took his great grandfather's watch to be mended and was asked: 'Have you checked the battery?

The Times

When complete strangers sent their manuscripts to Henry James to read, he replied:
  'I shall lose no time in reading your book.'

The Times

Thriller writer Ken Follett told Simon Hoggart about the time he was crossing a busy street with Jeffrey Archer when they were nearly run over.

Follett said to Archer that the headline would have been on the lines of 'Flower of British Literature Mown Down'.

Archer replied: 'Yes – and it would add "Jeffrey Archer was with him."'

Guardian

The *Daily Express* reported the 'sad fact that in Britain today there is a severe shortage of Gorgons... women who could stop a gang of marauding hoodies with a withering glance at 100 paces'.

Jennifer Selway sang their praises in a *Daily Express* article citing:
  • **Giles's umbrella-wielding cartoon Grandma**
  • **Margaret Rutherford as Miss Marple**
  • **Hattie Jacques' gimlet-eyed matron**

- Fanny Cradock – a Gorgon de cuisine, resembling a man in drag
- Coronation Street's Ena Sharples holding court in the Rovers Return
- Margaret Thatcher's handbagging skills
- Mothers-in-law (Les Dawson's epitaph for his being 'Gone but not forgiven')

Daily Express

A Portsmouth couple won £2.25 million on the Lottery and refused to move from their flat – in order to stay near their favourite bingo hall.

Independent on Sunday

Among books prized by antiquarian booksellers are:
- *The Haunted House* by Hugo First
- Criminal Life – Reminiscences of 42 years As a Police Officer by Superintendent Charles Bent
- *Drummer Dick's Discharge*
- *Flashes from the Welsh Pulpit*
- *Play with Your Own Marbles*
- *The Big Problem with Small Organs*
- *Scouts in Bondage*
- *The History of Concrete Roofing*
- *You Can Make a Stradivarius*
- *The Girl from Big Horn Country*
- *Piles for Civil Engineers*

- *The New-Poor Cookery Book* – a 1932 volume suggesting menus for down-at-heel households having to get by with only two maids

Daily Telegraph

Spring came early in 2007 and some flowers bloomed and faded before Easter. To avoid disappointing those enthusiasts who visit the Lake District to walk amidst

Wordsworth's hosts of golden daffodils, a holiday site at Lake Windermere was planting daffs made from plastic and silk... hoping 'that guests would not notice the difference.'

Daily Telegraph

The *Daily Mail*'s science editor Michael Hanlon describes as 'utter tosh' many of the myths which so many people so firmly believe:

- Lemmings commit suicide en masse.
- Lightning never strikes in the same place twice. In fact lightning strikes many locations over and over again – high trees, tall buildings, mountain tops – and lightning conductors.
- No two snowflakes are identical.
- Women have a higher pain threshold than men.
- When it is very cold, it cannot snow. (Try telling this to a Siberian.)

Daily Mail

Noel Coward bought his house in Switzerland sight unseen and said: 'It was advertised as having 37 hectares. I didn't realise until I got there that they were all vertical.'

Daily Telegraph

Artist David Hensel, 64, of East Grinstead, was delighted when his latest sculpture was selected by the Royal Academy for the 2006 Summer Exhibition. It was called One Day Closer to Paradise and was of a laughing head on a slate plinth.

Unfortunately the head and the plinth were packed separately for safe transit and the work was judged as two separate pieces.

The plinth was judged worthy of display. The head was stored away to be collected by the artist.

One of the experts responsible for choosing the plinth said he thought it was good example of minimalist art – '...a quirky little piece. We were puzzled by it and that's why we liked it'.

Artist Hensel commented: 'I had to have a laugh – but I would rather have had my sculpture there.'

He had originally hoped to sell the piece for £3,640 – but now believes he can sell the plinth separately for a higher sum. 'It has become art because it was chosen by these eminent artists,' he said.

Lots of newspapers had fun with this one.

A series of letters in *The Times* discussed the question 'What is an intellectual?' Among the offerings were:

- A person who can listen to the William Tell overture and not think of the Lone Ranger.
- A man who visits a strip club and watches the audience.
- Someone who, when left alone in a room with a woolly tea cosy, resists the urge to put it on his head.

A further letter claimed:

- Knowing that a tomato is a fruit is intelligence. Not putting it in a fruit salad is wisdom.

The Times

The fondue set, the staple of 1970s dinner parties, has been voted the least-used household appliance. Two thirds of them are put away and rarely got out again.

Also high up on the least-used list:

- Ice cream makers (second)
- Keep fit videos (third)
- Foot spas (fourth)

These are followed by games consoles, electric fans, back massagers, toasted sandwich makers and exercise bikes.

A survey by Pricerunners.co.uk found Britain's kitchen cupboards, lofts and understairs spaces cluttered with £2.5 billion's worth of barely used appliances and gadgets.

Daily Telegraph

Despite the findings of the Pricerunners' survey, people remain convinced of the usefulness of gadgets on the list. A *Daily Telegraph* editorial points out that they provide the uninspired with ideas for Aunt Jessie's birthday – and Aunt Jessie with something for the car boot sale... And where would eBay be without such items?

Daily Telegraph

It seems that more and more people no longer believe that you can do it if you B&Q it. Busy modern folk are abandoning DIY for GSI and DIFM (Get Someone In to Do It For Me). Half a dozen surveys describe a young generation of hapless householders – half cannot hang wallpaper and a quarter cannot sew a hem or wire a plug.

The Times reported on what it called 'the acme of GSI' when a professional handyman was called in to saw a chopping board in half because 'it wouldn't fit in the dishwasher.'

The Times

May 1 is the unofficial start of the DIY season, and the Royal Society for the Prevention of Accidents reminds us that 200,000 people required hospital treatment after accidents working at home.

Daily Telegraph

Hero worship was the name of the game when England celebrated the 200th anniversary of Nelson's victory at Trafalgar in 2005. It seemed that nobody cared about the dark side of the adored national icon.

But on page twenty-one of *The Times* on 19 October 2005, there was an article saying: 'Nelson's faults yawn every bit as wide as his virtues. Vain, self-seeking, silly, brazen, cruel, shameless – those were some of the kinder epithets hurled at him during his lifetime. Political cartoonists of the day were merciless. They poked fun at his love affair with Lady Hamilton, his social climbing, his pompous habit of parading in public dressed in all his medals.'

Nevertheless, the article continues: 'In some ways his misdemeanours make him more real. Unlike Wellington, he is a rounded human being. We do not hold his tantrums or his petty jealousies against him. We admire the way he cocks a snook at society. Nelson's flaws have enhanced rather than eroded his reputation as a supreme leader.'

The Times

Actor Michael Simkins complains about autograph hunters who hang around stage doors asking for as many as six autographs – for selling on eBay.

The Times

A survey by Hippowaste Refuse Disposal revealed some of the strange items which found their way to rubbish dumps:

- £200,000 worth of takings from a travel agency, packed in black plastic bin bags
- The secret blueprints of a proposed new aircraft carrier for the Royal Navy
- A pet tortoise contentedly hibernating in a green recycling bin
- The entire contents of a man's wardrobe, including dinner jacket and golf clubs (dumped by an outraged wife who found out her husband was cheating on her)
- A collection of twenty-five years of the Beano comic
- A suitcase full of skulls and other human bones (from absent-minded staff at a biology lab)
- A mattress stuffed with £5,000 in banknotes

Guardian

Jean Swann, of Northampton, remembers that many years ago a pair of gypsies called at her parents' house. They were carrying a baby and were given some of Jean's baby clothes.

The next time the gypsies were seen they were playing a barrel organ in the High Street – with a monkey sitting on top dressed in Jean's baby outfit.

Daily Mail

An average £3,744 worth of belongings are lost in a lifetime through lending items to friends.

Cornhill Direct poll, *Daily Telegraph*

Jeffrey Bernard Is Unwell, Keith Waterhouse's 1989 play about Soho's engaging dipsomaniac, reopened at the Garrick Theatre in June 2006 before a first night audience liberally sprinkled with Bernard fanatics who lapped up his quips and quiddities, such as: 'Soho is a place which welcomes you with open arms and legs.'

Evening Standard

Professor Joad said that a crossword is a device for making intelligent people think they are not wasting their time.

The Times

Janet Forse, a 49-year-old divorcée from Lydney, Gloucestershire, has complained to her local trading standards office about a dating agency. She was looking for 'a rugged, employed, fun-loving, non-smoking, educated, semi-professional, financially secure male aged between 40 and 55 with a good sense of humour and his own home.'

What she got were a succession of unsuitables who were variously unemployed, drunk, shy, badly dressed, lived in a caravan or skinny.

She claims that all eight blind dates provided were so disappointing that 'not even Cilla Black' would have tried to foist them on her.

The Times

Mrs Nancy MacPhee, of Bonnyrigg, Midlothian, gave her five-year-old son money to buy ice cream cones from a van visiting their street. On his way back he dropped one and said: 'Sorry, Mum, I dropped yours.'

Daily Mail

In his column 'btw' in the *Independent*, Sholto Byrnes tells of a friend who came across the autobiography of former Attorney General Lord Rawlinson in a secondhand bookshop.

A sticker pricing the volume at 50p lay in unfortunate proximity to the book's title: *Price Too High*.

Independent

Isabel Beeton was Britain's first domestic goddess and her *Book of Household Management* remains a housekeeping bible to this day.

She caught syphilis from her husband on their honeymoon and died aged 28.

There is no evidence to suggest that Mrs Beeton was interested in cooking, and she appears to have been a plagiarist who copied down other people's recipes and passed them off as her own. She was not a cook at all. She was a writer – and a light-fingered one at that.

Excerpts from *The Short Life and Long Times* of Mrs Beeton, by Kathryn Hughes, published by Fourth Estate, *Daily Mail*

A long and serious article in *The Times* Section 2 on whether men's brains and women's are different had a light-hearted introduction which said 'An entire industry of books, films, keyfobs and stand-up comedians can be mined from the subject':

Q: *Why is psychoanalysis quicker for men than for women?*
A: Because when its time to go back to childhood, he's already there.

Q: *Why does a man have a hole in his penis?*
A: So the air can get to his brain.

Q: *What's the main difference between women and men?*
A: Women can use sex to get what they want. Man can't because sex IS what they want.

Q: *How many men does it take to change a toilet roll?*
A: We don't know because it's never happened.

The Times

It's described as the ultimate test for a robot – assemble an Ikea bookcase.

Sunday Times

While scientists are scratching their heads over this one, art student Kieren Jones, 22, has created a fully functioning crossbow from a set of Ikea clothes hangers and also turned an Ikea chair into a sledge.

Sunday Times

The *Guardian Diary* launched a competition to 'Win-a-bottle-of-Posh-'n'-Becks' great-new-perfume -if-you-can-tell-us-why-the-hell-you-want it.'

A contender said his excuse was that his cat had just peed on the carpet.

Guardian

After Alistair Fellows, 43, of Burton on Trent, survived being struck by lightning. It was reported that he had previously:

- **Narrowly escaped electrocution after cutting through a power cable**
- **Broken his skull (twice)**
- **Been hit by a runaway lorry**
- **Had a toothbrush surgically removed from his ear**

Guardian diarist Jon Henley signed off his report with: 'We can only wish him luck.'

Guardian

Dinner lady Trish Emson won £1.7 million on the Lottery and bought a £47,000 caravan to live in on a site near Cleethorpes, Lincolnshire.

'Why would I want to live in a mansion or a posh hotel?' she said, pointing out that the caravan site had 'crazy golf and bingo, which I go to with my friends if we're not at the amusement arcades with the kids.'

Sunday Times/Daily Mirror

All Aladdin's magic was unable to help the chap chosen to play his genie in the Gloucester Operatic and Dramatic Society's 2006 pantomime.

When Aladdin rubbed his lamp the 23-stone performer chosen for the role failed on two counts. The lift on which was to magic him onto the stage was not up to the job – and his waist was too big to go through the trap door.

The Times

Marlene Dietrich lost a pearl and gold earring while riding Blackpool's Big Dipper roller coaster in 1934. It has been found, 73 years later, by workmen draining the lake under the Dipper. They also found three sets of false teeth, a glass eye, a bedraggled toupée, three dolls, a bra and £85 in small change.

(One can understand how most of these items might have flown off during a white-knuckle roller coaster ride – but how did the bra get there?)

Daily Mail

The number 13 is the one that's been drawn least in the National Lottery. Number 38 has turned up most often, followed by 25 and 31.

Independent on Sunday

In January 2007 a tiny flat in Chelsea – no bigger than a championship snooker table – was up for sale at £170,000 (and needing a further £30,000 spent on it). Amid headlines about it not being big enough to swing a cat in, *The Times* had a leader saying that to call it a flat 'stretches the boundaries of language'. It went on to give examples of estate agents' legendary claims:

- Stunning rooftop views – it is seven flights up the stairs
- Fashionable décor – fashionable in 1972
- Lends itself to reconfiguration by an imaginative buyer – the bedrooms are in the garden shed
- A fragrant home – it is above a takeaway
- Must be seen to be appreciated – must be seen to be believed

The Times

That jolly character Michelin Man – voted the advertising icon of the last century – is to become a mere shadow of himself in these weight-conscious days.

The company's marketing people have decided that he must 'lose some of his flab' for 21st-century audiences.

The fat fellow dates back to 1888 and is being slimmed down 'to keep up with changes in society'.

Daily Mail

Antony and Cleopatra were a long way from being Egypt's most glamour couple. Their portraits on 2,000-year-old coins show that she was a plain Jane with a pointy nose and thin lips. He had bulging eyes and a hook nose.

Historian Andrew Roberts debunks other bizarre tall stories that have been passed down from generation to generation:

- Boudica's chariot wheels were not fitted with scythes.
- Napoleon Bonaparte did not say 'Not tonight, Josephine.'
- The Philistines were not uncultured.
- Marie Antoinette did not say 'Let them eat cake.'
- Roman galleys were not rowed by slaves.
- Pirates did not make prisoners walk the plank.
- Richard III was not a hunchback.

Daily Mail

The Wick Royal British Legion Scotland Pipe Band will issue all its members with earplugs after the music at one of its practice sessions was recorded at 122 decibels – two decibels louder than a small plane. In a fact box,

The Times also showed that a train horn reaches 130 decibels, a lawnmower 95 and a barking dog 80.

The Times

It used to be *Times* readers who rushed to tell the world that they had heard the first cuckoo. Times change and in 2007 we had Andrew Cuthbert alerting the *Guardian* that he had spotted the first bare midriff of spring in March.

Guardian

'Infamy! Infamy! They've all got it in for me!' Kenneth Williams uttered the words in the 1964 film *Carry On Cleo*. It was voted the funniest film one-liner in a poll by Sky Movies Comedy.

Also high on the list was Groucho Marx in *Duck Soup* (1933) saying: 'Remember you're fighting for this woman's honour, which is probably more than she ever did.'

Daily Telegraph

The *Sun* invited its White Van Man readers to submit their jokes for a charity book entitled White Van Wit. Samples included:

- A wife asks her husband why he is studying their marriage certificate and he says he can't find the expiry date.
- What do you call a man who knows where her husband is every night? A widow.

- What's the difference between the England football team and a tea bag? A tea bag stays in the cup longer.

Sun

Simon Hoggart on second-hand bookshops: 'There should be a pungent and musty aroma... A sulky cat asleep on the only chair... A proprietor guarding a chipped mug of tea and who hates parting with the stock... like a dad seeing his son off for military service and not wanting to cry.'

Guardian

The Publishers wish to acknowledge the
following publications:

Daily Mail
Daily Express
The Times
Daily Telegraph
Sun
Guardian
Financial Times
Independent
Scotsman
Metro
News of the World
Independent on Sunday
Sunday Telegraph
Observer Magazine
Observer Food Magazine
(OFM)
Sunday Mercury
London Review of Books
The Press Gazette
Reader's Digest
Catholic Herald
Private Eye
Economist
Yorkshire Post
Birmingham Evening Mail
Newcastle Advertiser
Newcastle Evening Chronicle
Liverpool Daily Post
Evening Post, Leeds
Brighton Argus

Sheffield General Cemetery
    Trust Magazine
Coventry Evening Telegraph
Colchester Evening Gazette
Tamworth Times
Halifax Courier
Henley Standard
West Sussex Gazette
Western Morning News
Western Mail
Oban Times
Eastbourne & District
    Advertiser
Seaford Friday Ad
Cumberland News
Scunthorpe Target
Shropshire Star
Tandridge Chronicle
Radio Times
New Scientist
Country Life
BBC Olive magazine
Journal of Sexual Medicine
Adult Learners' Week
Focus magazine
Cambria magazine
Dogs Today
BBC News
Surrey Online
Teletext

You Couldn't Make It Up

BY JACK CROSSLEY

YOU COULDN'T MAKE IT UP

'What a wonderful collection of old rubbish'
– Keith Waterhouse

In his many years as a newspaper journalist, the inimitable Jack Crossley has stumbled upon literally thousands of wonderful little anecdotes that you really wouldn't believe if you hadn't seen them written down in black and white. He has compiled them into this irresistible book of essential whimsy.

Sir, While clearing the house of a deceased aunt we found a box labelled, correctly: 'Pieces of string too short to keep.'

Genuine letter to *The Times*

Our story about a fire being started by an old pouffe at No. 7 Douglas Cottages, as reported last week, referred to an item of furniture and not the owner, Mr Donnie McArthur.

Apology that appeared in the *Dunoon Observer*

ISBN 1 84454 005 7
£6.99

You Really Couldn't Make It Up

MORE
HILARIOUS
BIZARRE-BUT-TRUE
STORIES FROM AROUND
BRITAIN

BY JACK CROSSLEY

YOU REALLY COULDN'T MAKE IT UP

After the runaway success of *You Couldn't Make It Up*, Jack Crossley presents his second cornucopia of wonderful anecdotes and strange goings-on from around the British Isles.

A Northumberland woman saw a TV tip about putting crabs in the fridge for 20 minutes before cooking them. She followed the advice – and the crabs ate ten choc ices.
Independent on Sunday

At the age of 105 Dolly Jackson, of Hereford, said that she started smoking when she was 14 – but was giving it up to help her live longer.
News of the World

ISBN 1 84454 078 2
£7.99

YOU ABSOLUTELY COULDN'T MAKE IT UP

'All human life is here in twenty-six chapters of mirth ranging from British eccentricity to legal lunacy to royal flushes to saucy seaside humour' – Simon Jenkins

From the mad machinations of the British bureaucrat to the one-off antics of barmy eccentrics who pepper our towns and cities, Jack Crossley's skill is in hacking a way through this bewildering forest of the pompous, predictable, polemical, political and pure pap to pick out the stories that really matter. The ones that make us laugh.

A sex survey claims that an orgasm burns off 27 calories, but faking it uses 160.

Sun

A bookie in Putney, London, hired a feng shui expert to redesign its betting shop – because punters kept on winning.

Mirror

ISBN 1 84454 180 0
£7.99

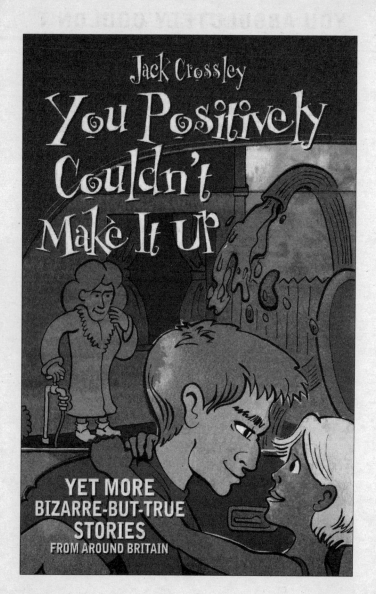

Jack Crossley

You Positively Couldn't Make It Up

**YET MORE
BIZARRE-BUT-TRUE
STORIES**
FROM AROUND BRITAIN

YOU POSITIVELY COULDN'T MAKE IT UP

'Most sequels deteriorate. Jack Crossley is the only writer whose serial sequels get funnier every year. His books make me laugh out loud' – Celia Haddon of the *Daily Telegraph*

The fourth and most fantastic collection yet of strange-but-true everyday absurdities selected by the seasoned connoisseur of British eccentricity.

Sign on a garage door next to Harpsden Church near Henley-on-Thames: 'Thou shalt not park in thy neighbour's space.'

Henley Standard

David Gethyn-Jones was driving out of Bristol Airport when the car behind shunted into him. The driver explained that he had been distracted by a large sign reading: 'Bristol International wishes you a safe onward journey.'

Daily Mail

ISBN 1 84454 314 5
£7.99